D0425179

Also by Ronald Rood

GOOD THINGS ARE HAPPENING

HOW DO YOU SPANK A PORCUPINE?

LOON IN MY BATHTUB

WILD BROTHER

HUNDRED ACRE WELCOME

LAND ALIVE

WHO WAKES THE GROUNDHOG?

MAY I KEEP THIS CLAM, MOTHER? IT FOLLOWED ME HOME.

IT'S GOING TO STING ME!

Juvenile Books

HOW AND WHY BOOK OF ANTS AND BEES

HOW AND WHY BOOK OF BUTTERFLIES AND MOTHS

HOW AND WHY BOOK OF INSECTS

WONDER BOOK OF INSECTS WE KNOW

BEES, BUGS AND BEETLES

THE SEA AND ITS WONDERFUL CREATURES

ANIMAL CHAMPIONS

RONALD ROOD

Possum in the Parking Lot

WITH ILLUSTRATIONS BY
CARRYE E. SCHENK

SIMON AND SCHUSTER • NEW YORK

PUBLISHED BY SIMON AND SCHUSTER
A DIVISION OF GULF & WESTERN CORPORATION
SIMON & SCHUSTER BUILDING
ROCKEFELLER CENTER
1230 AVENUE OF THE AMERICAS
NEW YORK, NEW YORK 10020

DESIGNED BY EVE METZ
MANUFACTURED IN THE UNITED STATES OF AMERICA

1 2 3 4 5 6 7 8 9 10

LIBRARY OF CONGRESS CATALOGING IN PUBLICATION DATA
ISBN 0-671-22588-X
ROOD, RONALD N.
POSSUM IN THE PARKING LOT.
1. URBAN ECOLOGY (BIOLOGY) I. TITLE.
QH541.5.C6R66 574.90973'2 77-1429

Contents

Here's How It All Began . . .

"If it wasn't so serious," Howard Black continued, "it'd be funny. Reminds me of a movie cartoon I once saw. The kid in the cartoon started after a whole flock of mosquitoes with a fly swatter. He got 'em all, too—except one. That one was too quick for him. It escaped every time."

He grinned at the thought. "The kid went after that mosquito so fast that all you could see was a blur with fly swatters in all directions. And at the end, there's the kid all tuckered out—with the mosquito drifting to a landing on the tip of his nose."

We had been wondering how long ago the last genuine buffalo had been seen here in the upstate New York city that bore the animal's name. Thinking about the demise of the eastern bison, we listed a number of other former natives of the Buffalo area: the coyote and timber wolf, for instance, and the passenger pigeon.

It was at this point that Howard remembered the cartoon. In a way, he suggested, we were like that kid with the fly swatter—getting rid of every living thing as fast as we could in our passion for progress. But then, like the 'skeeter that wouldn't be squashed, some maverick plant or animal would poke right up again.

Considering it further, we realized that there was a hefty number of nonconformists that refused to retire peacefully when we came on the scene. Preoccupied as people are with rare and threatened plant and animal species, we may overlook those living things that are doing quite well, thank you, in spite of us. Or even because of us.

As if they had heard us talking, a dozen pigeons fluttered down to the sidewalk in front of his tiny porch. No shortage of pigeons, that was sure.

In the vacant lot across the street a dried weed jiggled as some unseen nibbler took an experimental bite. Such activity probably released a few seeds that might be caught and spread by a friendly breeze. So the weed and its small animal neighbors were doing fine, too. In fact, as we thought and talked about them, we realized that there were, indeed, living things sharing our fortunes even here, right near the center of the city.

Some of these survivors seem to be getting along almost too well. Ask a park superintendent what he thinks about pigeons. The noisy congregations of starlings along the front of City Hall must be the century's best success story. Brother Rat in his walls and cellars is also very much at home—to say nothing of assorted other critters, some of which we've come to regard as pests.

There are other living things that have fitted in more comfortably, at least from our standpoint. Some, coming in from rural areas, apparently like what they find and have decided to stay. Others were here all the time and have merely moved over to make a place for people. They stand bravely along the edges of our streets, stoutly gloss over the scars of construction and destruction, and bring welcome color, motion and sound to the man-made world of the city.

We thought about these little-known, little-appreciated

neighbors of the taxi driver, the street vendor and the office worker. In many cases, we figured, a couple of starlings on a fire escape or a seedling sprouting in a rain gutter might be the only remaining contact the city dweller had with the long-forgotten wilderness. To such people a sparrow in a hedge might be as important as a fawn in a thicket would be to a farmer.

Supposing, then, that these wild urbanites have not only a place but a function in our man-made world—where would one look for them? What magic resiliency has enabled them to adapt to smog and noise and postage-stamp parks instead of the miles of quiet forest they once knew? How can they, among the dismal list of faded animal and plant populations, get by with a culvert for a cave or a rubbish heap for a refuge? And what might we do for such enterprising plants and valiant animals by way of encouragement?

We talked about them a few minutes more and finally decided that their stories might be not only interesting, but important as well. After all, they have solved a lot of problems; perhaps it would help to find out how they've done it.

"Maybe," Howard concluded pointedly, "someone ought to write a book about them."

"Maybe," I countered hastily, seeking to avoid a direct hit, "somebody already has."

With this little exchange we went our separate ways. The pigeons left the sidewalk, Howard went back to his delivery truck, and I returned to my woods and fields in the Green Mountains of Vermont. But our conversation had started me thinking, and I checked through libraries in the next few weeks.

There were plenty of lists of plants and animals and how to identify them, of course. There were books that told how to attract wildlife to your home—if you lived in the country.

But little seemed to deal directly with the city. So, perhaps Howard did have a point. I'd think about it.

Now, a couple of years later, I have thought some more. And this is the result. Here they are, those living things that struggle to keep up with us, poking brave green leaves out of old auto tires, and peering soberly from the tops of garbage cans. Some of them you will have seen; others you may not recognize at first. And now and again it may be a bit startling when you meet them face to face.

But then, since it was their land before it was ours, *they* must be a bit startled when they meet *you*.

1·An Ailanthus Grows in Brooklyn

WE WERE WALKING down one of the city's busiest streets, Peg and I. Horns blared, taxis rattled, buses pulled in and out of traffic. I stopped at a little sidewalk shop, bought a snack to tide us over until lunch, and then looked around for a place to throw the empty wrapper.

"Here," said my wife, indicating a trash bin on the street corner, "toss it here. Maybe it'll be compost for that little plant."

I dutifully wadded the piece of paper and dropped it into the container. Then we both considered the living occupant of that trash bin. It was but a tiny seedling, the offspring of some unseen tree, bravely lifting two little green leaves up through the cigarette butts and candy wrappers. There had been enough moisture in the rubbish to enable it to germinate; now its roots searched down through the litter for the good soil that should be there. Its cotyledons, or primary leaves, still had a bit of substance left. They would provide a few days' more energy while the leaves struggled up toward the sun that visited that street corner about two hours daily.

The traffic light changed from red to green. Half a hundred

people surged forward, sweeping us along with them. Soon the little seedling was several blocks away.

That fleeting moment occurred more than a year ago. Doubtless the seedling found itself dumped and compacted by the garbage truck just a few days after we passed by; the trash bin was long overdue for emptying. And even if that bin somehow got overlooked, the little plant's fate would have been much the same, for there was nothing in the way of soil or food to sustain it for long. But at least it had tried.

It was really no great surprise to see that plant. They're always dropping down on the city like a slow, quiet rain—these pioneer seeds and fruit that seek to colonize our streets, roofs and sidewalks. Off they go, whisked away from the parent tree by a sudden breeze. The flying samaras of maple and ash, the little brown snowflakes of elm and birch, the odd one-winged whirlybirds of basswood or linden launch out on their perilous mission. They may actually gain altitude for the first few moments of their flight as the breeze encounters a wall or a building and rises over the obstruction. Then, kept aloft by the currents that often rise from heated pavements, they may travel halfway across the city. Looking down from the highest windows in midtown, the office worker can often see little patches of green growing at random in the gravel of city rooftops—the homes of airborne seeds.

Sometimes they have plenty of company. Capricious drafts pick up all kinds of loads. One time a friend and I were sitting at a picnic table in a little park when a sudden gust of wind caught a newspaper that was lying on a lawnchair. It lifted the paper, played with it for a moment, and then took it up over the trees and out of sight. Along with the newspaper, in a minicyclone, went dust, straws and leaves.

Most likely a few bits of life were borne aloft, too: half a dozen seeds, perhaps, or an unwilling ant or beetle. In fact, samples taken from the snows of the Himalayas high above timber line have yielded bits of moss, twigs of trees, spiders, and even caterpillars. Transplanted from their homeland, they were carried about until, in time, the wind left them high and dry, and frozen forever.

Some seeds get a different ride. Suppose a bird alights to look for food in a berry patch. The seeds of berries, the kernels of sumac and the pits of wild cherries are tough little motes of life. They pass unharmed through a bird's digestive system. Deposited later in the bird's droppings, the seeds break out of their resistant coats wherever they find themselves—anywhere from the edge of town to the corner of Third and Main.

Animals may carry seeds about in their fur. In fact, you may have given the fortunes of the plant world a boost yourself. On a weekend in the country—or when you took a shortcut through a vacant lot—you may have blundered right through a good collection of burrs and stickers. Perhaps your clothing was tweedy enough to collect a few seeds the way an angora sweater attracts lint. Later, discovering these unexpected guests, you pull them off and drop them right there. This, of course, fits you right into the whole scheme, especially if you're helpful enough to discard those burrs where there's enough debris so they might have a chance.

Yes, seeds can get around, all right. The problem is what they do after they arrive. They still have to germinate, find good soil, enough sunlight, adequate water. A full-sized elm may scatter half a million seeds in a single day, but most of them are doomed to failure. They end up in windblown piles on the street, or as tiny deltas and moraines along the edges of gutters and rainfall rivers. The tufted parachutes of cottonwood trees drift down upon you like an airborne division. They get in your eyes and nose, cling to your clothes or lie in wait on the seat of the bus. Such locations are scarcely fertile ground for new cottonwoods, and they usually end up as candidates for a whisk broom or as inhabitants of a vacuum cleaner.

Now and again, however, some lucky pioneer finds things

more hospitable. The two prime requirements for sprouting—warmth and moisture—combine with enough air to support its growth, at least for a little while. The tiny bit of life first puts down an infant root to anchor it in this friendly spot; then it sends green explorers upward toward the light. And if the fates are really kind, it may actually begin to grow.

Then, too, a tree may be a sort of landscaping leftover. As the crews survey and scrape and build, some bit of greenery may be overlooked. Perhaps it's in a remote corner of a building lot, or at the edge of a forgotten pile of debris. There it stands on the sidelines, safe as long as nobody notices it.

Well, almost safe. It often takes more than luck to insure its livelihood. Squatters' rights may not be enough. Fumes and waste from the activities of its new human neighbors and their machinery may do it in. Draining or filling of land may upset its water supply. The sudden disappearance of its neighbors with their shade, their influence on soil conditions, their shelter from wind and erosion—these losses may be more than it can endure. And, of course, if it's all alone in a sea of humanity and pets, it may be overwhelmed with attention. People collect its twigs to add to a centerpiece. Youthful Daniel Boones with jackknives leave their mark. Visiting dogs investigate it with deep and abiding interest, and then leave *their* mark, too.

Some trees, however, can stand the gaff. In fact, they may bear up under it so well that they actually thrive on it. Such durable species may be bypassed by a careful builder on purpose, or planted on the new plot so that Sylvan Estates lives up to its name—at least, faintly. With a bit of prying into the contents of nearby vacant lots or waste places along the edges of streets and alleys, you can discover a few of these favored kinds for yourself. Then, recognizing them, you may be able to help them along in their growth—or, if you get to know the right people, you may even be able to dig up just the tree for that little spot in your own yard.

Such native-grown plants, by the way, may be superior to the ones you get in a nursery. Lest the commercial growers cry in anguish, however, I hasten to emphasize that word *may*. A tree grown in a certain climate and moved just a few blocks is all attuned to local weather. It may be toughened to local diseases too—although there's also a good chance that it may harbor some malady that no nursery would give an inch of growing room. In addition, the rugged life it has led could have made it more sturdy than nursery stock, even if it ends up looking like a brush pile on a stick.

Then, too, it may well be a species liked by wildlife. After all, it was planted there somehow in the first place—perhaps by a bird that ate its fruit, or a squirrel that buried the seed. So, in adopting it, you may be starting a minirefuge of your own. Thus, you stand to reap an added reward of wildlife and their antics.

Bill Gleeson, a friend of mine in Glenview, on the outskirts of Chicago, noticed several small trees that produced attractive blossoms every spring. They were growing at the edge of a sandpit near his home. He liked the white flowers with their thin, half-inch petals, plus the oval, fine-toothed leaves. He was intrigued by the smooth, gray bark with the vertical dark streaking that, as he said, reminded him of an undertaker's trousers. They apparently did not belong to anyone, but grew up as they were among the overturned cars and an extinct piano. So Bill dug up several of their seedlings and relocated them in his tiny back yard.

That was twenty years ago. Now he has a three-tree grove of shadbush, or sarvistree (*Amelanchier* species), plus an unscheduled bonus: an edible crop of reddish-purple fruit the size of blueberries. Robins, starlings, sparrows seem to appear from nowhere, right in the city when the berries ripen in June. Sometimes his children beat the birds to the feast; they manage to pick enough so that Bill's wife, Peggy, can make a Juneberry pie.

Bill and Peggy know their plants. Yet there are a number of other trees that almost anybody can identify. Rather than launch into the delights of do-it-yourself forestry for the next hundred pages, however, I'll mention just a few. The ones you will meet are included because of unusual interest, appearance, or downright usefulness.

Take the tree in the title of this chapter, for instance. There are plenty of other kinds among the trees that grow in Brooklyn, but Betty Smith's novel has helped the ailanthus to gain some of the attention it deserves. Too long has it been dismissed as a slum tree because of its ability to take root in almost any vacant lot. Its virtue lies in that very imperturbability that allows it to grow right where the soot and grime seem thickest.

Gifted with fluttery, airborne samaras, whose flattened red-green-yellow "wings" surround the central seed, *Ailanthus altissima*—the "tree of heaven"—can drift to new horizons down the block with almost any puff of wind. Once the cornflakelike samara has settled to earth, it soon graces the spot with new growth. The compound leaves, looking something like gigantic ferns, may be more than three feet long. They bear as many as thirty leaflets arranged in pairs along a central stem, with a single leaflet at the tip.

It's not just a seeming fondness for waste places that gives *Ailanthus* its somewhat tarnished reputation, however. The branches are apt to be weak and brittle, for its growth is fast and weedy. One of those sudden city gusts may crack a limb, which hangs loosely until the neighborhood kids break it off, strip its leaves, and give it its final moment of glory in a game of street hockey. Then, too, the foliage has an unpleasant odor when crushed. So does the bark, as well as the yellow-green staminate flowers with their clouds of pollen.

The pistillate (female) clusters smell much better, however. Since the two types of flowers are borne on separate trees, an ailanthus of the right sex may be a welcome neighbor—considering that, like any neighbor, it has its shortcomings.

Grant it its drawbacks, and in a single year, on the trashiest lot in the neighborhood, it will be an eight-foot living umbrella where none had been raised before. Weak and smelly though it is, this eighteenth-century Asiatic immigrant may at last allow the city dweller to feast—visually—on some greenery other than the imported vegetables in the local supermarket.

Another tree of surprising endurance is the American elm. It scarcely seems to notice the bustle going on around it. Drive into Boston, Washington or Detroit, and observe the change in plant life. As you leave the expressways and approach the inner city, few trees seem to withstand the wind, the roar, the gases that swirl along the roadway. Even the grass is dry and discouraged. But chances are that, of the remaining trees you see, a number of them will be elms.

Not tall elms, perhaps, or whole ones; the rush of the city and the unscheduled visits of wayward automobiles take their toll. But even if some battle-scarred veteran looks as if it has been the victim of a concerted attack of a troop of beavers, it is unmistakably an elm. As long as there are any limbs at all, they tend to grow gently upward and outward, parting from the main trunk as if the whole tree were a large vase. If the trunk has been snapped off completely, new growth still sprouts from the broken stump.

Drop off the busy highway onto one of the side streets and *Ulmus americana* will be there, too. Now you can note the features of the twigs and leaves. Each twig has a slightly zigzag appearance, due to the alternate arrangement of the leaves—one on this side, then one on that. The leaves themselves are a bit lopsided, with one half larger than the other. Rough on top, downy beneath, they are oval with doubly-saw-toothed edges ("a tooth on a tooth," as my forestry professor told us) and softly pointed tips. Its fuzzy green blossoms of early spring soon give rise to thousands of waferlike seeds. These seeds scatter like confetti with every breeze.

As you look at this denizen of our modern metropolis, consider its illustrious past. Stately and dignified, the tree was used by early pioneers to grace their towns and cities beyond its natural limits that reached from the Atlantic to the Rockies. So tough and durable was its cross-grained wood that hundreds of covered wagons creaked westward on wheel hubs of elm. Ribs and timbers of ships were made of it. Trains roared westward over railroad ties of elm. Furniture, butter tubs, barrel staves—almost anywhere a rugged, nonsplitting wood was needed, elm was often the first choice.

Even the bark found a number of uses. The Indians stripped it from young branches and used it for baskets and snowshoes. Twisted and braided, it made strong, supple ropes. Larger pieces were used in canoe building. The pioneers learned to chew the bark of the related slippery elm as a cough remedy, and slippery-elm lozenges are still a soothing treat for a raw, raspy throat.

In the past several decades we have inflicted undeserved hard times on our old friend. Elm timber imported from Europe brought with it the fungus of a disease that soon infected nearby trees. Carried by bark beetles, it choked the tiny vessels in living elm wood, effectively girdling the tree. Dutch elm disease, as it is now called, has ravished elms wherever it has found them, and it has left entire cities with gaunt skeletons where once were tree-shaded avenues.

One dubious distinction I wish I had not had was to be among the first to discover that the fatal malady had invaded as far as Waterbury, Connecticut, I believe it was in 1940. We found it in a struggling little elm alongside a railroad track by a factory. Had the elm not been so hardy in the face

Elm Tree

of industrial fumes, it might not have been there to receive an infection from the nearby railroad. By the time we got the unhappy tree dug up and burned, its neighbors were infected. Then, shortly, America became preoccupied with World War II, and Dutch elm disease was left to its own insidious devices.

There is a hopeful note, however. John Hansel, Executive Director of the Elm Research Institute in Harrisville, New Hampshire, assures me that the means is now at hand to save individual trees. "The fungicide is not a cure-all," he added, "nor is it cheap. But when you have a two-hundred-year-old giant that arches over half a city block, it's well worth the cost and effort to save it."

A general breakthrough, John feels, can happen at any time; they're that close to a solution. If so, the noble American elm can go back to shrugging off smog and cinders without the indignity of fighting an enemy within at the same time. And the hardy little saplings may continue to stand at their roadsides and back alleys and add a touch of scenery for the commuter, the driver of the delivery van, and the sanitary engineer on that growling, clanking garbage truck with the insatiable appetite.

It's easy to establish an elm of your own. Those waferlike seeds sprout readily in a pot of soil if they're interred about twice their thickness below the surface. This, by the way, is a good rule of thumb for determining how deep any seed should be planted—twice its diameter. Thus, you'd bury large seeds at a greater depth than small ones. Water the pot so the soil stays slightly moist but not wet; the elm seedling should poke aboveground in a week or ten days.

If you dig up a small tree, its roots will likely have about the same spread as the top—another general rule to help you determine how large the underground portion of a plant may be. Obviously you won't be able to take such a cluster of earth; so dig out as much as you can conveniently handle. Keep the roots moist and intact. Then, to put roots and upper parts back into balance, prune off about half the branches after it has been planted. An elm withstands such a performance well; its roots are so numerous and hardy that they will endure all but the most botched-up spadework.

The best time to relocate a plant is when it is dormant—after leaf-fall in autumn, or before new growth in the spring. If you can do your transplanting in two operations, so much the better. Your first activity would be to root-prune the tree or shrub several months before you move it. Cut straight down into the soil in a circle with your shovel; this severs the outreaching roots and forces new growth to form beneath the main body of the plant. Then, when you come along later with the second step of digging up and hauling away you've got a solid clump of vigorous new roots. Your plant is now ready to go—unless some unsympathetic construction crew has bulldozed away your prize in the meantime.

One more hint: try, if possible, to face the plant in the same direction in its new location. If its main growth is lined up north and south, say, turn it in the same direction when you set it in the hole. Of course, an apartment building may be in the way of perfect alignment, or passersby may take an unfriendly view of a limb that sweeps out over their line of march at eye level. In such cases you'll have to sandwich the new arrival in as well as you can.

If all you have is an outside stairway or a window ledge, you can still try your hand at fire-escape forestry—consistent with safety regulations. And don't forget the safety of people on the street below. Put a few chunks of old crockery, or even pieces of broken glass, in the bottom of a three-pound coffee tin for drainage. Add soil and seedling. Prune the little plant as it grows, and pinch off the terminal buds at the ends of the branches. The result will be your own bushy version of the Japanese *bonsai*, and you too will have a tree growing in Brooklyn.

Elm makes a good candidate for such vest-pocket landscaping; it goes along with almost any scene. But there are several other trees you might like to try—or, at least, learn to call by name. Among these are the willows, poplars, birches, maples, sycamore, locusts, wild cherries and oaks. You'll also see trees that were originally planted for shade and decoration, but whose offspring have gone native, so to speak. There they stand among their poor relations, eluding the gardener and the grounds superintendent, living in sooty splendor on the wrong side of the tracks.

Willows, poplars and birches resemble one another in having the familiar "pussy willow" flowers, or catkins, in spring. The catkins of birches are brown and woody when dormant. Then they lengthen and hang down almost like yellowish caterpillars. Poplars often have large catkins; in fact, those of the cottonwood may droop as much as six inches, giving it the name of "necklace tree." Willow catkins are somewhat more sedate, at least at first, but may become exuberant as the weather warms up. They reach an inch or more in length and offer their pollen to bees, flies and the sensitive noses of hay-fever buffs.

You can spot most willows by their slender, tapered leaves—from the narrow four-inch-long blades of weeping willow to the somewhat broader and shorter foliage of pussy willow. The leaves are borne alternately, often at intervals of several inches. The twigs are apt to be flexible and—well—willowy. Their bark is often quite yellow—almost a canary color in weeping willows, especially as winter turns to spring. And there they stand, at the entrance to a culvert or along an eroded gully, soaking up what moisture they can obtain and adding their touch of grace and color to the dingy landscape.

Willows are often a snap to plant. I remember helping my

grandfather start a willow fence on his farm one spring day. We merely broke off a few dozen willow wands as the snow was melting and poked them into the water-soaked ground. In a couple of weeks the catkins emerged, followed shortly by the leaves. The wands took root, and today there's a line of willows fifty feet tall, right there in Harwinton, Connecticut.

One word of caution if you try to start a willow for yourself: Its roots have a great affinity for moisture, and they'll seek out buried water pipes. Then, if they gain entrance through a joint or crack, they may clog the pipe, and you're in trouble with the landlord.

Some poplars, like willows, may prefer slightly moist feet. Cottonwoods, with their deeply furrowed bark and bountiful growth, sometimes have roots that reach half the length of a football field in their search for water. Lombardy poplars, those tall columnar trees that often line water courses and ditches, may keep right on sprouting when the land is filled and leveled. Their adventuresome roots, exploring underground, find the hidden moisture and pass it along to the distant leaves and shoots.

Two other poplars, the quaking aspen and the bigtoothed poplar, are less fussy about living conditions. In fact, they are often the first trees to colonize burned-over ground, bringing a quick and welcome mantle to cover the dreary scars of fire.

You can tell almost any poplar, even in the dark, if you can get a hand on one or two of its leaves. The leaf stem, or petiole, is flattened at right angles to the leaf blade. Thus, when you try to twirl the leaf between your fingers, it is difficult, if not impossible. Such a slender petiole tends to buckle and twist with every little movement of air, imparting a shimmering appearance to the tree. The quaking aspen has petioles that are almost paper-thin, so its leaves are in almost constant motion: hence its familiar name.

One legend has it that the road followed by Christ on the way to Calvary was lined with aspens. Overcome by the horrible sight, the trees began to quiver with apprehension, and have quivered ever since. Today the peculiar property of the leaves is indicated in the tree's scientific name, *Populus tremuloides*—"trembling poplar."

Many poplar leaves are triangular in shape, like the Greek letter, *delta*. Hence, if you couldn't tell the cottonwood from its wispy parachutes that spoil the appearance of your best blue suit, you might recognize it from its peculiar leaves. Here, too, the scientific name fits: *Populus deltoides*—"delta-leaved poplar."

Although scientific names are often obscure, at least one other poplar bears its technical handle perfectly—the bigtooth poplar, or *Populus grandidentata*. The windborne seeds of this adventurer can eke out a living on parched, fire-ravaged ground. They sprout by the city dump or on the lot where the old warehouse burned.

Birches usually join the poplars in these pioneering efforts. Gray birch—often mistakenly called "white birch" but differing from it in having triangular leaves like a poplar (hence gray birch's scientific name, *Betula populifolia*)—grows for miles along some of the roadways approaching downtown Montreal. Its cousin, the white or paper birch (*Betula papyrifera*), has leaves that tend to be more oval in outline.

In case it is winter, when there are no leaves to help tell the difference betwen the two white-barked species, take things in your own hands—literally. Rub the bark; if it's a gray birch there'll be nothing on your hand. If it's a true white birch, however, your palm will be covered with a chalky, white powder. And there you have the white, "powder," or canoe birch. This last name indicates the importance of great sheets of the peelable bark in the days of early settlers, Amerindians and the French *voyageurs*.

If you have played with wooden toys, they may have rolled on wheels of paper birch. Birch clothespins hung the washing on Grandma's line, and birch spools held her sewing thread. Today, white birch may bracket both ends of a good meal: the salad bowl to start it and the toothpick to end it.

And what of gray birch? Does it spend its career merely as a stand-in for its illustrious cousin?

Hardly. Quick-growing, able to endure drought and a degree of pollution, it seeds itself along the banks of new highways and home sites, anchoring the soil. Many a fast-buck artist has thrown together a few tacky houses, bulldozed the area clean, and escaped with his winnings. Behind him he leaves the faithful gray birch, like Horatio at the bridge, to cover up for him.

Not only does the birch stabilize the earth and serve as a volunteer ornamental, but it is also valuable as a nurse tree. Providing shade and shelter, it forms a canopy under which other plants may get their start. Then, since gray birch is relatively short-lived anyway, it may die away before the mortgage is paid, retiring in favor of its more permanent protégés.

Other birches—variously called red, silver, yellow, blue and black, after the color of the glossy bark—are sometimes left over from the original forest. They receive their change in station with something less than enthusiasm. Seldom can they compete successfully with their new neighbors—plant, animal and human. However, if protected and cherished, individual trees may continue in good health for years. You can usually identify any of these birches by a pronounced minty flavor to the twigs and young bark. In fact, black birch is distilled to make oil of wintergreen, while its sap is used in birch beer.

Twigs of distinctive flavor belong to the cherry tribe, too. You can find wild cherries along the brushy edge of almost any vacant lot. However, if you have never sniffed a cherry twig, prepare for a surprise. The odor is strongly like that of bitter almonds. So is the taste, if you are that adventuresome. But lest you be tempted to use a cherry twig for flavoring, I will tell you about the Webbs' prize ram.

Kenneth Webb and his wife, Susan, ran several summer camps, known as the Farm and Wilderness Camps, in Plymouth, Vermont. Unlike "Silent Cal" Coolidge, also from Plymouth, Ken is a ready conversationalist. Many a youngster's camp experience has been enriched by an evening around the fire, listening to Ken spin a few of his many yarns.

One time, however, he did not say enough. A purebred ram, to be used for breeding on the farm, was staked out in the meadow at the end of a long chain. Ken had cautioned the campers not to let him eat the shrubbery at the edge of the field, but he had neglected to tell them why.

"It was my fault," he told me, "for not explaining about the poison that builds up in wilted cherry foliage. So I really had nobody to blame but myself. The kids got careless after we had the ram a few days, and staked him where he could wander through the bushes."

Fresh cherry browse can be eaten by grazing animals in limited quantities with no harm at all. Wilted leaves, however, such as those torn and crushed by the chain of the ram as it clambered around in the fence row, concentrate the almond-smelling substance enormously in their bruised tissues. That substance—prussic acid—is an aqueous solution of cyanide gas. "And by the time we discovered him," Ken said, "he was breathing his last. In a few more minutes he was done for."

The children were beside themselves with remorse. They had loved the ram in the few days he had been on the farm, and they took up a collection toward a replacement. But purebred rams of the right blood lines aren't that easy to find.

"So our sheep and wool program went into limbo for a while," Ken told me.

Then he chuckled. "We almost lost our cook, too. Nobody told him of the loss, and he had the misfortune to come up with fresh cherry pie for dessert that night. He picked over the cherries, pitted every one by hand, and served the pie right out of the oven. Nobody'd touch it, and he darn near walked off the job, right there."

Lest you go out to that overgrown patch of brush and rip every wild cherry out by the roots, however, recall that it was *wilted* foliage that killed the ram. Fresh leaves and twigs have little more than the smell of the deadly gas.

A forester friend of mine takes groups of people on natural-history walks right on the outskirts of Philadelphia, encouraging them to use all their senses in identifying trees—sight, smell, taste, even touch and hearing as they experience the sharp "snap" in breaking the twigs of spruce and spicebush. "And you should see the look on their faces," he says, "when I tell them the 'almond' taste of the twigs they're chewing is really hydrogen cyanide."

Besides that faint cyanide flavor, wild cherry can be told by its white, five-petaled flowers, usually borne in clusters. The dark-green oval leaves are characteristic. So is the shiny red or black bark that turns scaly with age. Cherry also may fall prey to black knot, a fungus that produces typical dark masses on twigs and limbs. The small fruit with their hard inner pits can be made into jelly and are eagerly sought by birds. Common black, or rum, cherry (*Prunus serotina*) may produce abundant fruit that quickly ferments when ripe. Then on a warm August day, you may witness a flock of birds teetering on the limbs, smack in the middle of a black-cherry jag.

Cherry trees need abundant sunlight. They're so attractive to birds and wild mammals that it's worth the effort to set out a couple if you have the space. Learn the location of others of their kind, too; they're a good place to look for all kinds of wildlife.

In contrast to the sun-loving cherry trees, many maples can grow in all but the densest shade. Thus you may find them at the rear of buildings or coming up through the branches of other trees. Our Vermont state tree, the sugar maple (*Acer saccharum*) is fine in this respect. I've seen its grayish bark, brownish twigs, maple-leaf leaves and two-winged "keys," or samaras, thriving with no care at all in Boston and in several parks of New York City.

Last spring I stood but a couple of blocks away from the Yale Bowl in New Haven and watched the ancient art of "sugaring" as practiced by industrious honeybees that were busy gathering the sap from the broken branch of a sugar maple. They would concentrate it to about forty times its original sweetness, just as the Vermonter boils forty gallons of sap down to produce a gallon of syrup.

Most maples have those typical lobed leaves borne opposite each other in pairs along the stem. The leaves of red maple (*Acer rubrum*) have jagged edges and sharp V-clefts between the lobes. Sugar-maple leaves are less jagged, with rounded clefts. So are the leaves of the Norway maple (*Acer platanoides*), one of the commonest "city trees" all over America.

Often planted in large cement "planters" on city streets, or growing from a tiny square of soil in the midst of acres of sidewalk, the Norway maple is an import from the Old World that is very much at home in the New. No place seems too "downtown" for this tree with its large leaves, evenly ribbed bark, and the springtime sprays of greenish-yellow flowers. The abundant samaras, their wings pointing out in opposite directions, make fine toy helicopters to toss into the air. Take a few home, plant in your well-drained tin can, water them carefully every other day, and you'll soon have a little maple grove of your own.

There's one maple that seemingly isn't a maple at all. This is the ash-leaved maple, or box elder (*Acer negundo*). Like the ash trees that occasionally find their way to the metropolis or linger on when the city limits expand, the box elder bears compound leaves with three to seven variably edged leaflets. But it's a true maple, however, as you can see when the two-winged samaras ripen in summer. Produced in great quantity, they hang long after the leaves have fallen, providing food all winter for sparrows, finches and grosbeaks. Try a box elder in your back yard if you need quick shade. It's not fussy, grows rapidly, and while those thousands of seeds may be a bit untidy, they'll hold a welcome mat out for birds all winter.

Sycamore, or buttonball (*Platanus occidentalis*), looks like a maple that has been daubed with whitewash. Its leaves have a decided maple look, but they are borne alternately, rather than in the opposite fashion of maples. The outer bark is green or brown, while the inner bark is whitish. As the tree grows the outer layer cracks and peels off, showing patches of the inner bark and giving the tree a piebald look. The spherical seed clusters hang all winter, like brownish Ping-Pong balls at the end of four-inch wires.

Sycamore can live in the grimiest of conditions, as long as there's plenty of moisture. It has grown for years along the banks of the Naugatuck River in Connecticut, a stream that used to be little more than an oversized sewer. A hurricane in the middle 50's flooded the river, scoured away the banks, and left embarrassing factory outwashes and domestic toilet drains poking out all the way from the Massachusetts border to Long Island Sound. Chastened, the residents of a score of towns cleaned up the river. Today the water is clearer, fish and insects are coming back, and lesser plant life has joined the durable sycamores that weathered it all and are still there.

Less fussy about the availability of water, but equally unconcerned about the tendency of moisture to rot most wood, are the locusts. The black locust (*Robinia pseudoacacia*) and the honey locust (*Gleditsia triacanthos*) are, therefore, fashioned into fence posts, railroad ties and other uses where resistance to rot is important. You can find these tall trees growing almost anywhere: along cindery railroad rights-of-way, up through the roofs of dilapidated buildings, in discouraging situations of all kinds.

Both locusts have compound leaves of many leaflets, plus flattened pods that show their relationship to beans and peas of the legume family. Honey-locust pods bear a pulp that separates the seeds. It is sweet to taste, as many a street urchin has learned in a lucky find during a game of sandlot baseball. Black-locust pods are less edible—at least from our standpoint—but they hang on the tree all winter and provide food for wildlife. The pealike blossoms of both species are eagerly sought by bees. They make a fragrant bouquet too—if you can get them. Thorns on black-locust twigs make for prickly picking, while those of the honey locust are so jumbled and spiny along the trunk and limbs that you would be better off trying to shinny up a cactus.

Quite the opposite of the prickly locusts are the clean, sturdy limbs of the oaks. An oak with a horizontal limb makes a good "swing tree" for anything from an old tire on a rope to a fancy chain-hung, polished metal seat. Members of a widespread family, the half hundred American oaks may live as solitary monarchs in a field or as residents of a natural woody condominium right there behind the "Choice Business Location" sign. Their leaves vary widely, too—from the typical lobed structures of white, black and red oaks to the simple green ovals of live oaks in the South. Generally, the various light-barked white oaks, of which *Quercus alba* is a common type, have rounded lobes. The leaves of the black oaks—*Quercus velutina*—are tipped with a short bristle on each lobe.

No matter what the color of their bark or the shape of their leaves, the oaks bear one feature in common—those peculiar structures known as acorns. Carried about by squirrels and then forgotten, an acorn may present the neighborhood with a new little seedling far from the parent tree. Acorns can float along through storm sewers. They find lodging in the pockets of youngsters. They may stay there for months, along with all the other valuables that accompany kids on their adventures through life. Small wonder, then, that the mighty oaks that have long figured in shipbuilding, barrelmaking, flooring, and a hundred other uses where a hard, tough wood was needed, still share in much of our lives today.

Acorns are fun to grow. They are large enough to handle and lift and poke around to see if they have sprouted yet. Let them remain outside in winter's cold to "cure," and then half-bury them in soil. Water them every other day, like a growing plant, and then one morning you'll see a fine, robust primary root sending out an exploring tip. It feels around, finds which way is down, and plummets into the earth. The cotyledons, or primary leaves, shed the tough acorn coat, and soon produce the first pair of true leaves. These open, spread, and soon proudly proclaim "oak." All in all, it is a nice, satisfactory tree.

Other trees may add an unexpected, welcome touch. Trashy, sandy soil will discourage most plants, but pines often thrive in such places. Hemlock, that graceful evergreen with the drooping, flattened sprays of foliage and the top that curves over—instead of standing up stiffly, as in the pines—will grow in deepest shade. Both pine and hemlock make good transplants into spots that would overwhelm more finicky trees.

Then there are those trees that escape. The catalpa, with its dark-brown, curving, pencillike pods, for instance, optimistically tries out new locations if it gets a chance. American basswood may raise its heart-shaped leaves in almost any American city, just as its close relative, the linden, does on those shady avenues in Europe. Horse chestnuts trot off on adventures of their own, just as they did long before Longfellow's village smithy stood under the spreading [horse-] chestnut tree. Their palmately compound leaves, with leaflets radiating out from the petiole like the fingers of a hand, are joined by the whitish flower clusters in spring and the prickly burrs in the fall. Their relative, the buckeye, is so common in the Midwest that it's the Ohio state tree.

True chestnut, by the way, has all but disappeared. The devastating chestnut blight of half a century ago eliminated this most valuable hardwood tree. It still struggles here and there, however. You may see the long, straplike, deeply saw-toothed leaves on sprouts that grow from the dead stumps until they get eight or ten feet high. Then, just as you begin to nourish the hope that this tree will be healthy, along comes the blight and lays it low again.

Those courageous, half-sized chestnut sprouts are often more like shrubs than trees. And this brings up a question: what's the difference between a tree and a shrub, anyway? Well, go back to the start of this chapter. Take that shadbush, or sarvistree, for instance. The latter name accords it a lofty station in life, while the former relegates it to a lesser level. One name must be right and the other wrong. Right?

Not necessarily. On some soils and near either extreme of its range (southern Canada, say, or down on the Gulf Coast) the shad*bush* fits the definition of a shrub: low, brushy, with several branchlike stems rising from the ground. In other areas it becomes quite a respectable tree, rising on a single trunk to forty feet or more. And in between, such as my boyhood home in Connecticut, the tree and the shrub may grow side by side.

You have probably noted such differences yourself. Think

of a New England town green where a balsam fir (*Abies balsamea*) occupies an honored central spot. Each December it is festooned with Christmas lights hung at high jeopardy by the local Rotarians, the Scouts or the firemen with their motorized extension ladders. If you hike to the top of some nearby mountain, however, it is hard to believe that you are seeing the same species. The balsam firs are stunted by wind and cold, a hundred years old and no taller than you are. In one place the fir is clearly a tree, while in the other it looks like a shrub. And somewhere in between you cannot tell what it is.

Perhaps the best thing is just to say that there are other woody plants than those tall ones known as trees. Some of them are bushy; others are like slender whips; still others are clinging vines. Then, too, they may combine all three habits of growth—like poison ivy, for instance.

Poison ivy is sensitive to light and soil and growing conditions. Its abundant foliage may blanket an old house foundation with a mantle of glossy green. It may become a foot-high mat in an open woodland. And it looks like an ornamental vine as it grows innocently up the trunk of that big swing tree at the edge of the neighborhood playground.

Caring little whether we welcome it or not, *Toxicodendron radicans* may make itself at home almost anywhere in temperate North America, excluding deserts and deep woods. In more southerly parts of its range it is joined by its close cousin, the poison oak (*T. quercifolium*). Both species look much the same, except for poison oak's more deeply lobed leaves. The best way to deal with either of these pesky plants is to follow the admonition: "Leaflets three; let it be." Each leaf, it seems, is composed of three leaflets borne on short stems of their own. The foliage is usually shiny and, when young in springtime, is often a glossy red that turns to green as the plant matures.

Whether climbing as vines on trees and buildings or creeping along as low, weak-stemmed plants where there's nothing to support them, poison ivy and poison oak bear small greenish-white or yellowish flowers that are followed by tan or white berries. Their bushy cousin, the poison sumac (*T. vernix*), has similar flowers and fruit, but you'll seldom blunder into it. Poison sumac prefers swampy areas, while poison ivy and poison oak grow in drier places such as picnic grounds, old stone walls, the edges of golf courses, and other helpful locations.

Apparently we humans are the only creatures so abundantly blessed with an allergy to poison ivy. I remember watching in awe as our family cow consumed great mouthfuls of the stuff along the stone wall of our farm in Connecticut. Her milk didn't hurt a bit, either. Apparently those capacious innards nullified the poison. And many birds gobble poison-ivy berries on one old trashy lot, say, and then fly to another lot. There, in the fullness of time, they void the seeds in their droppings—complete with a little pat of fertilizer to give them a good boost in life.

Incidentally, you may not actually need to touch poison ivy or others of its ilk to get a case of dermatitis. The smoke from burning plants may contain droplets of the resinous sap. Thus a Saturday bonfire may result in a Sunday rash when you thought you were perfectly safe. In fact, if you got a good morning start you may reap the benefits, so to speak, that same evening. With some people the allergy takes only a few hours to make itself known. Sometimes a dog or cat romping through the foliage may bring home some of the sap on its fur. Even garden tools can serve as carriers, especially if you're highly sensitive.

But the plant *is* attractive. It grows gallantly and seems to thrive on a diet of trash and litter. It can cover a deserted car or an abandoned rubbish pile in a single season. Given half a dozen years it will climb up a fire-blackened tree or a forgotten utility pole, replacing grimness with greenery. So you have to give it credit for something.

Some lucky people are immune to poison ivy. Immunity varies from time to time, however, so best treat it always with healthy respect. There are several ways to demonstrate this respect. First, of course, is to avoid contact. Then, if you discover you blithely wandered through poison ivy country, carefully remove the clothing to prevent more trouble. A scrub with hot soapy water may remove any bits of dried sap, although such treatment usually arrives too late to get you away scot-free. Apparently the pernicious plant does its work in the first few minutes of exposure. It usually takes hours for you to get the full benefit of it, so don't rejoice too much after a suspected dose of the stuff until at least a couple of days have passed.

Calamine lotion is still an old standby for poison-ivy rash. Pain-deadening salves and lotions will also help. My personal treatment consists of steaming hot compresses; with a good case of ivy I may end up practically parboiled, but at least it stops that itching. Then, too, you can get "shots" against the poison, but they're more of a prevention than a cure.

Scratching does not spread the rash, by the way. All those watery blisters are merely your own reaction to that earlier exposure. You may get an infection by scratching, of course, but with most people poison ivy is little more than a memory after several days. Luckily, you probably will not have a first-person meeting with poison sumac; its effects may linger for a couple of weeks.

But how about the sumac that you see growing along railroad embankments and around dumps? Yes, it is a sumac. Those compound leaves and clannish growth will lead it to take over an area completely, if given half a chance. How do you know it's not poisonous? Just take a look at the twigs.

Most likely they are thick and fuzzy. The twigs of the poisonous species are smoother and more slender. If you have ever seen the antlers of a deer while they are developing "in the velvet," you will understand the name of this city species: staghorn sumac (*Rhus typhina*).

Then, too, the staghorn sumac has red berries. Borne in fuzzy upright clusters at the tips of the branches, they're quite different from the whitish drooping berries of their rascally cousin. There are also a couple of other species of sumac you may encounter, but their red berries will likewise put your worries to rest. By the way, a simple trick to bring a bit of life to some tired old gravel pit or even an embarrassing spot in your own yard is to drop a few of these red sumac seeds on the soil. Scuff them in with your foot, and let nature do the rest. Sumac is not the most beautiful shrub, but it grows rapidly and endures everything but a flamethrower. It provides an added reward in the numbers of birds and other wildlife that visit it. It also turns scarlet red in the fall.

Since the fuzzy seed cluster remains most of the winter, it makes an ideal hiding place for spiders, caterpillars and other tiny creatures. Birds—even the kinds that do not normally eat seeds—inspect each cluster carefully for these slumbering tidbits.

Even without the visits of wildlife those shrubs that hold their fruit in winter can bring a welcome touch to a drab neighborhood. Nearly every plant can be propagated by burying a few of its seeds or fruit. Allow them to remain all winter on the twig, or on the outside of your window in a coarse-mesh bag where they get the wind and rain. Many species will not germinate without this ripening process. Plant them in the spring, however, and they will grow as easily as those plants in the seed catalogues apparently do.

When you discover one of those scraggly, thorny small trees of hawthorn or thorn apple (*Crataegus*) in some disreputable spot you can filch a few of its small applelike "haws" for yourself. Leave them outside for the winter. Then plant them where you had despaired of getting anything to grow. In a few years you may be rewarded with attractive white blooms, thorny twigs that make ideal fortresses for bird nests, and a few of those reddish haws that add a little color to your winter scene.

There are many other shrubs that are quite obviously "making it" right there in town, even as others are leaving the scene forever. There is the flowering dogwood (*Cornus florida*), for instance. This is a small tree with opposite branching, globular flower buds that look like miniature gray onions. In the spring they produce showy white blossoms. There is its roadside cousin, the red osier dogwood (*C. stolonifera*), whose purplish to blood-red twigs along roadsides have been called "the veins of spring," because of their striking color against late winter snows.

There are several species of roses (*Rosa*) with their fragrant blooms, persistent winter "rose hips" as emergency food for birds and wildlife—and greenish briars to remind you, as you wander incautiously in a vacant lot, that the whole world isn't totally civilized yet. There is also sassafras (*Sassafras varifolium*) with its yellowish-green or reddish-green twigs. Sassafras leaves may be oval, mitten-shaped or three-lobed. Its aromatic tissues are sometimes used to make root beer.

Sweet fern (*Comptonia peregrina*) and bayberry (*Myrica pennsylvanica*) inhabit sandy and worn-out soil. Sweet fern looks like fern leaves borne on twiggy shrubs; hence its name. Bits of its aromatic foliage used to be tied in the forelocks of horses to keep the flies away. Bayberry can usually be spotted by those gray, waxy berries borne in twos or threes along the stem. It is these berries that provide wax for bayberry candles.

Add to these the grapes, blueberries, blackberries and raspberries that persist, or start new colonies, where we forgot to dig and fill and pave and build. Tack on two more edibles: the American barberry (*Berberis canadensis*) and elderberry (*Sambucus canadensis*). The prickly barberry keeps breaking ranks from its well-trimmed hedges—with the help of birds, mice and chipmunks—and goes tripping over the landscape. There, in autumn, its scarlet fruit hangs in clusters, ready to supply you with jelly or even a seedy pie as it did your forebears of the nineteenth century. Elderberry's large, flat-topped clusters of tiny white flowers give way to purplish-black fruit in late summer, ready for jam, jelly or wine. The pithy center of its twigs could easily be hollowed out with a wire to form sap spouts for maple-sugar making. They also made ideal peashooters to lighten the boredom of a day at school. Or so I've heard.

There is one shrub that may even be worth cold, hard cash —not for itself, necessarily, but for what it can tell you. This is the bushy tree known as the alder (*Alnus* species). The common alder (*A. serrulata*) and the rough alder (*A. rugosa*) are similar in having oval, saw-toothed leaves. They have smooth bark with raised white pores, or lenticels, and pendant male catkins that hang gracefully like tiny pigtails, while the female flowers look like half-inch pine cones.

Alder grows rapidly, usually forming clumps or clusters from a common base. The wood has a weak structure; you can often snap a broomstick-sized piece with your bare hands—something you would find hard to do with a broomstick.

Now for the profit in getting to know an alder: it is seldom far from water. If you are contemplating a new home in, say, Sunny Vista Estates, and there is evidence of alders about, better contemplate some more. The place might become Swampy Vista during a prolonged rainy spell, and you could find yourself with all the joys of a basement that lets the water in, and a bathroom that won't let it out.

Even if hidden by tons of fill, topped by lawn and streets

and houses and dubbed Arid Acres by an optimistic builder, a wet spot may still be wet underneath it all. A swamp or marsh, it seems, is a reflection of the general height of underground water in the area. Even if the swamp is filled in, the surrounding water level, or water table, remains the same. It just takes longer for the water to seep through, that's all.

I remember the first home Peg and I ever owned. It was in a Long Island development a few miles from New York City. We had lived there only a few weeks of our first winter when we made an absorbing discovery, so to speak: our toilet was taking longer to flush. An inquiry informed us that all our neighbors were similarly favored. The surface of Long Island is but a few feet above the water table, at best, and locating several dozen homes in a former swamp hadn't helped at all. With all those postwar babies and automatic washing machines adding daily to the underground supply, an actual dome of water was building up faster than it could seep off into the already-saturated ground.

As a result, a new industry grew and thrived in the area: septic-tank pumping. The trucks made regular rounds of the homes every few weeks, just like the meter reader. Then your plumbing worked for a while. It was an expense and a nuisance, even if it did create a few more jobs. And what irked me, when I took time to notice them, were the alders standing at the north and west edge of our postwar paradise, as if to say "I told you so."

On the other hand, if you're looking for water, a clump of alders can be a welcome sight. Since they usually are shallow-rooted they will indicate moisture at or near the surface. Perhaps there's more where that came from, too. So, alders can be important either as a warning or a promise.

Then, too, knowing that they are so fond of moisture, you can populate an unsightly wet spot with alders. Peg and I visited some Akron, Ohio, friends whose dishwasher and washing machine join forces to supply a hidden underground catch basin in their back yard. The overflow from the basin gives periodic sustenance to a grove of alders. They are getting along well, detergents and all, even though the wildly fluctuating water supply leaps from drought to deluge.

There are many more trees and shrubs that can bring life and color to an otherwise hopeless landscape. To list them all would be next to impossible, for nearly every plant brought in as a docile captive for somebody's well-tended grounds may suddenly decide to rough it half a city away.

Indeed, I once took part in a study of the woody plants within the limits of Washington, D.C. We did not count those that were obviously set out and cared for—just the species that had voluntarily helped to brighten up the nation's capital. It was a government study and it ran out of funds, but I recall that a list made by a friend and myself totaled over sixty species.

So, it seems, as long as there is the smallest spot where a plant might possibly lodge, that spot eventually may be occupied. Then, if you happen to take a look, as Peg and I did, you may find yourself confronted with a little seedling, struggling upward and doing its best to brighten the corner where you are.

2·*Dauntless Dandelions*

WHAT IS A WEED, ANYWAY?

Ask a golfer and you'll probably learn that a weed could be almost any plant except good, green grass. But ask a gardener and he might name grass first of all.

James Russell Lowell called a weed a flower in disguise. Ralph Waldo Emerson decided that a weed was a plant whose virtues had not been discovered. One dictionary on my shelves asserts that a weed is "an ugly plant," while another calls it "a plant that grows to excess on cultivated ground."

Our botany class in college pondered the question. Whether a plant was a weed, we realized, depended not only on what the plant was, but *where*. As one student pointed out, a cornstalk was fine on an Iowa farm, "but not"—indicating the baseball field visible beyond our laboratory windows—"out there by second base."

Finally we hit upon a definition. The same idea is given one way or another in botany books, seed catalogues and gardening magazines. A weed, we decided, was merely a plant out of place.

The plants, of course, labor under no such restrictions. The right place, most of the time, would be the spot where they can eke out a living. To a sticky mistletoe berry, clinging to a bird's beak, that "right place" would be any tree limb where the bird wiped its bill. Thus its seed could germinate, invade the tissues of the tree, and produce the bushy, leather-leaved parasite in the middle of any forest—or city park—from southern New Jersey to the Gulf States. A sprig of mint, tossed out with somebody's julep, might be covered by enough wet soil to take root there behind the restaurant. And, before the days of the sanitary landfill, nearly every town dump had its complement of self-sown tomato and pumpkin and watermelon plants—the leftovers, as it were, from the meals of a whole village.

In fact, a great number of those hardy little plant volunteers known as weeds can be traced back to leftovers of one kind or another. Stand at an abandoned railroad yard or the edge of a street, and notice the plants that are growing there; struggling up amid the cinders and tin cans will be ragweed, plantain, grasses, wild mustard, clover, dock and dandelion—to name but a few. And nearly every one of them can be traced back to some time when they were tossed out in somebody's trash. Not yesterday's trash, either, but as long ago as that of the first pilgrims.

When those original settlers came to this country they found a land nearly blanketed with forests. One story has it that a squirrel, seeing the approach of a great sailing ship, became so frightened that it dashed up into the trees and kept running until it reached the Mississippi Valley. Such a fanciful tale yields this much truth, at least: almost everywhere in those early days there were trees, trees—nothing but trees.

Cattle and horses find slim pickings in the forest, so the pioneers sent back to Europe for supplies of hay. Sprinkled

STI
GROW
GREEN
WEED
KILLER

throughout that hay were the seeds of dock and daisy and buttercup and scores of other stowaway plants. Some of the seeds successfully ran the gauntlet of a bovine or equine alimentary canal. Others sifted down to the bottom of the manger, where they joined the straw and uneaten hay. From there they were used as bedding, passed along to the manure heap; and, come spring, the whole works was spread on the newly turned soil. Then, sure enough, the early farmer found that this wasn't such an inhospitable land, after all; there was something familiar about the landscape. Many of the weeds he had known back home were growing here too.

Added to such a fertile supply was another source of plants-out-of-place. This was the earth used as ballast in the holds of ships. Shoveled out at the end of its voyage, it was often hauled away in carts. It was used in gardens, complete with roots and seeds and half-smothered plants. Then, too, the pioneer homemakers brought carefully nutured herbs and spices for their pioneer gardens.

Years later, it became popular to bring to the New World those plants that have been named in the literature of the Old. So, if we hadn't already had onions and mint and nettles, our country soon would have sprouted them—for weren't they mentioned by the immortal Shakespeare himself?

Then, too, there is the collector's urge, in nearly every one of us, to save everything from stamps to seedy souvenirs of that trip abroad—and it is easy to see how plants can get around. Opportunists that they are, many of these plants have kept right on going long after their original benefactors have deserted them.

No, it's not hard to imagine a route by which that dandelion, say, made it to the tiny patch of soil alongside the supermarket. Indeed, the fluffy airborne seeds of *Taraxacum officinale* can go almost anywhere on earth. I've watched them drift past the window, right in Rockefeller Center, where Betsy Schenk and I sat and talked with our editor, Julie Houston, about this book. I have seen them get "caught" by the ferryboat as it headed away from the dock at Burlington and dance in the eddying backdraft of the boat all the way across Lake Champlain from Vermont to the shore at Port Kent, New York.

If you have ever tried to pull a dandelion up by the roots you know how it resists your efforts. That fleshy taproot, somewhat like a skinny carrot, makes an admirable anchor. It also makes a fine pantry. When times are good, it stores food manufactured by the leaves; when times are bad, it gives the food back to the plant. The leaves themselves, with their jagged edges, supposedly resemble a mouthful of wicked fangs; hence, the French name *dent-de-lion*, "lion's tooth."

One book on herbs points out that the dandelion "gilds both edges of the year" with its yellow blossoms. Even here in northern New England you can find the golden blooms bravely held to the waning sun in November, joyfully welcoming its return in February. Further south a friend who lives in Providence, Rhode Island, says that she can easily find dandelions at any time, even in the dead of winter. Snuggling up to the south side of a building for warmth, or sheltered in the corner between adjacent walls, the lion-hearted lion's tooth may never quit.

The plucky dandelion is but one of that large family of plants known as composites—so named because what seems to be a single flower is really a cluster of tiny blooms, a botanical bouquet. Other members of the family Compositae may be equally at home among the dregs of city life.

Take ragweed, for instance. This anathema to the hay-fever sufferer displays its spikes of tiny green composite flowers everywhere from the spaces between railroad ties to that corner lot where the old building was pulled down. Its scientific name, *Ambrosia*, which may bring to mind the drink of the gods by the same name, relates better to another godlike characteristic—*ambrotos*, which is Greek for "immortal." And there, if you can ever take your eyes away from the traffic long enough to watch the jagged foliage of the plant as it flutters wildly in the breeze from countless cars along an expressway at rush hour, you will see a plant with a name that really fits.

If you have pulled the two-pronged pitchforks of beggar's-ticks (*Bidens frondosa*) from your clothes, you've made the acquaintance of another composite. I've garnered an unintentional harvest of this yellow-flowered hitchhiker in many a vacant lot. Once I had to pull off the highway just outside the center of Toronto to fix a flat. The beggar's-ticks added their bit to the joys of getting down to meet a deflated tire on its own level.

Another come-along composite, the common burdock (*Arctium minus*) may grow in a bewildering tangle on that block where the high-rise apartment building never got off the ground. The tall, spreading stems of last year lurk all summer. Their furry-looking seed balls are ready to cling to a sweater or jacket—or even the hair of your arms—and go along with you in search of new worlds to conquer. This year's crop with its pinkish flowers comes up from among the huge basal, bitter-smelling leaves. The bristly receptacles of the flowers, when they mature, are abundantly able to replace the loss occasioned by your snagging of last year's harvest.

With the composites known as thistles, the whole plant is prickly: flowers, leaves and stems. If you have eaten artichokes, you may recall the tiny bristle that surmounts the tip of each edible scale. Artichokes, it seems, are giant, cultivated thistle buds. Their wild relatives, bearing such interesting names as pig thistle, cow thistle, and bull thistle, I'm told, are likewise edible if you can figure out how to eat them. Quite obviously the spines are to provide effective insurance against such a fate.

One of the most impressive performances I have seen was

that of a pet burro belonging to a friend we were visiting in Grand Junction, Colorado. The burro had broken its rope and wandered off during the night. The next day our friend received a phone call: would she come and get her burro? It was making itself at home just outside the fence of the Grand Junction Race Track. We piled into the car and drove the three miles to the track. And there was Eeyore, long ears slowly waving back and forth, placidly munching on thistles.

Like their cousins the dandelions, thistles set their offspring adrift on gossamer parachutes. Once these seedlike achenes have germinated, their sturdy roots may search many yards, if necessary, for water. So almost any patch of empty earth may become adorned with those outrageous plants with the soft shaving-brush blossoms.

Other armored pioneers endure where lesser species would be overwhelmed by the play of children and the romping of pets. Prickly lettuce (*Lactuca scariola*), growing as much as eight feet high, has yellow flowers on a craggy spike. The spike surmounts coarse, bristly, dandelionlike leaves. Break the leaf or stem of prickly lettuce and it oozes a milky sap. The sap has a mild anesthetic effect. Rub it on poison-ivy rash or a mosquito bite, or even the scratch you got from getting too familiar with prickly lettuce itself.

Several species of pigweed (*Amaranthus*) may appear in unexpected places. Their tiny greenish-purple flowers, crowded on a coarsely fuzzy spike, make unpleasant handling. However, the plant affords a welcome bit of green where otherwise there might be none. One species, the thorny amaranth (*A. spinosus*), bears a pair of spines in the axil where the oval-shaped leaves join the stem. An adventurer from South America, it has worked its way north through the years. I have found it along the cluttered banks of the Hudson not far from Albany, perhaps having jumped ship from a river barge.

If you've ever had a good burning, itching case of urticaria, known more familiarly as hives, you could probably guess what plant was meant by the botanical name *Urtica.* Sure enough, it's the nettle, whose scientific name comes from the Latin word *urere,* "to burn." And so the plant known commonly as a nettle declares in scientific jargon: "*Urtica*—I burn!"

All you need is a gentle touch, and you've been introduced. The spines of many nettles look like coarse hairs. In fact, the skin of a peach may seem more threatening than the fuzz on the leaves of some of these deceptive plants. A typical nettle needle is an exquisite little hypodermic, containing an irritant and capped with a fragile bulb. Brush against it, and you break the tiny bulb, leaving a jagged end, which immediately scratches you, helpfully dribbling out a tiny drop of its poison at the same time.

When Peg and I lived on Long Island we were on the outskirts of the metropolitan area of New York City. Having been brought up in the country, we wanted a vegetable garden. So, we spaded up a tiny plot about the size of half a dozen card tables and installed a few plants of lettuce, carrot and tomato. The neighbors were scandalized ("What? No lawn?"), and some of their offspring, never having seen a garden before, continued to use our back yard as a shortcut to the local playground.

We hated to put up unfriendly signs or a fence, but it was obvious that we would soon be done out of a harvest. However, we needn't have worried. A horde of nettles, moving in all by itself, created an effective barrier across the back and two sides of the garden. The waist-high plants with saw-toothed opposite leaves sprang up in a couple of weeks. From then on, those nettles took violent exception to any more such traffic. And we didn't lose a single friend, either.

Nettle flowers look somewhat like the spikes of some grasses: small, greenish, and borne in clusters. True grasses, of course, are of no relation to nettles—except that both are plants. Grasses fill in the spots where other plants may long since have given up. They grow right to the mouths of city tunnels. They cluster around the bases of bridges and guard the creosote-embalmed bodies of their gigantic tenth cousins, the trees, as the latter stand in pile-driven rows at the edge of a dock.

Grasses live an exhilarating career as cliff-hangers in the chinks of somebody's cement wall. They even add a modicum of success to a few million window boxes and flowerpots, for, after all, if grass will survive, won't something else grow too?

Ride along on the outskirts of almost any city in America where the pavement is raised above the swampy ground, and there you may see one of the world's most impressive wild grasses towering above the familiar cattails. Soaring as much as twenty feet in the air, the great plume grass, or wild "reed," keeps you company for miles. It grows along New Jersey's Garden State Parkway, for instance, or busy U.S. Route 1 from Maine to Florida. Peg and I once attended the Mardi Gras in New Orleans. One squadron of bicycles in the parade bore three spears of plume grass each, cut from a local bayou. The tufted flower heads of the grass looked like brownish-white ostrich feathers bobbing in the breeze ten feet above the street.

Plume grass, technically known as *Phragmites,* gets along without the formality of fruit or seeds. And it gets along very well, too. Creeping through the mud of a swamp or tidal flat, the underground rootstocks may travel as much as thirty feet, sending an exploratory shoot up for air and sunlight every yard or so. And they travel a lot farther than that thirty feet, too; you may find plume grass in almost any available ditch in the warmer parts of the world.

This grass almost seems to prefer the city. Or perhaps

more correctly, it can make a go of it where other swamp residents curl up in anguish. Roadside canals can be loaded with so many throwaways and discards that if a ditch were covered for a few centuries and then exhumed, it would be a perfect time capsule. Some future archaeologist may discover what we drank, smoked, chewed, wore, read, put in our cars, took out of our cars, swallowed to keep us awake, to put us to sleep, to add weight, to take it off—the evidence would all be there. And there too, amid the faint odor of petroleum, would be a fossil of plume grass, faithful in death as it was in life.

The smaller cousins of the giant reed are more typically grasslike in appearance. Many grasses are hard to sort out, even for a specialist, but they are generally alike in bearing those slender leaves that spring from a "collar" wrapped around the stem. It is the presence of this collar, rather than a firm attachment, that allows you to pull a sprig of grass gently from the sheath of its lower leaves, exposing a tender green tip that makes tasty chewing.

Some of the best of such nibbling is provided by that medium-high grass known as timothy. Answering to the technical name of *Phleum pratense,* timothy bears a cylindrical seed head that is about the length and diameter of a pencil stub without the point. One of the leftovers from the time of horse-drawn vehicles, timothy survives today along the roadways in hundreds of towns and cities. There it lingers like a nostalgic grad reluctant to leave the dear old alma mater.

Many other grasses—dozens, in fact—may border the street where you live. It is hard to say just how many species there might be. Grass seed travels far and wide. You scratch one mixture of it into your new lawn and spread another mixture out for the birds. That's ten or a dozen kinds of grass, right there. Your parakeet gets one formula, your canary another. There go a few more species when you toss the litter out. With today's emphasis on organic foods, even whole oats and wheat and barley—grasses all—go along in pockets and pouches for nibbling as a natural food snack. So they too may find their way to the street again.

And note that last word, "again." In the heyday of the horse, oats and other grains found daily use as feed. Scattered from the noontime nosebag, or passing safely through some hundred feet of innards, the resistant seeds lay on the pavement or the cobblestones, there to be sorted over by those cocky little gleaners, the city sparrows. In those times the sparrows were not as numerous or pesky as now, and people looked on them with indulgence. In fact, when the first horseless carriages came on the scene, bird lovers in many parts of America were outraged. Soon there would be no food on the street for their talkative little friends. "Sparrow killers!" they shouted after the departing contraption as it roared down the street.

There are still more grasses. These range from several species of foxtail, with their bearded heads and pleasant odor, to the sandbur (*Cenchrus*), whose semiprostrate jointed stems bear clusters of spiked seed cups. One botany book describes these delights of the sandlots as having seed heads composed of "spikelets subtended by an involucre of inflexible spines, and deciduous at maturity." This means, in plain language, that the wicked little burs drop off when ripe. There they lie, just waiting to make a brief acquaintance with one of the barefoot generation.

Your yard may play host to another relict of those days of the pilgrims. Crabgrass, that despair of fastidious lawnkeepers all over America, probably arrived in an early load of hay. It has been with us ever since, successfully making the transition from horses to horsepower, and living up to its common name as it spreads, flat and crablike, in many directions, from a central root.

It lives up to its scientific name, too: *Digitaria sanguinalis*—

the "ruddy little fingers." For the three or four fingerlike seedstalks are reddish in appearance. *Sanguine* also means "cheerful" or "buoyant." Those adjectives fit the sturdy plant, green as ever in a blistering August drought, while the rest of the lawn is parched and brown. Which brings up a question about crabgrass that either attests to my respect for the rugged plant or tarnishes any image I may have had as a meticulous home owner: why complain so bitterly about crabgrass? At least it's green, isn't it?

There are other grassy residents that may stand there by the bus stop, or gather like a little green island around a street sign, or shrug off the indignities that traditionally attend the fire hydrant in dog-loving America. Given a chance, they might grow up to be pasture grass, orchard grass, squirreltail, or Kentucky blue grass. Without the so-called fruiting heads, however, one species looks a great deal like another. Suffice it to say that they are just grass—glorious green grass. Stubbornly clinging to existence, their fibrous roots may thread through no more than a few handfuls of soil. As they go they extract every atom of nourishment from that soil. They cherish each droplet from your distant lawn sprinkler, every cooling rain and every splash from auto wheels through the puddle there by the curb.

Nowadays trucks carry bales of hay from farms right into the city—for horse shows, suburban riding stables and animals in zoos and parks. Those bales contain whatever was growing in the original meadow. Bumping along, they release chaff and seeds, which are thus planted by the road. Such a wayside "garden" may be hundreds of miles long before the hay reaches its destination. So the travels of the plants continue, winter and summer.

Some of the most attractive of our plants-out-of-place may thus be carried around, either by hay trucks or by clean-up crews that rake and shovel the roadsides. Red, white and hop clovers; their tall blue-flowered alfalfa cousin; the incredibly yellow-orange-colored blooms of the bird's-foot trefoil; and the common and crown vetch—these are among the relatives of the pea and bean that travel wherever we do.

Like the other members of the legume family, these species usually bear root nodules that teem with bacteria. These bacteria act on soil nitrogen, changing it to a form useful for the plants. Such a partnership allows a lupine, say, to thrive many miles from where its next-nearest brother or sister raises those attractive pinkish-blue blossoms.

The legumes are usually joined by many other plants that have dropped out along a line of march that may extend back for hundreds of miles—and hundreds of years. The composite known as chicory (*Cichorium intybus*) volunteers its dollar-sized flowers of azure blue at intervals on their waist-high ribbed stems. Its ground-up root is sometimes used as an additive to coffee, or even as a substitute. Its cousin, the yarrow, raises small, white, many-flowered heads above an aromatic mass of leaves whose finely cut appearance gives it another name, both common and scientific: milfoil (*Achillea millefolium*). Yarrow may have escaped from great-great-grandmother's herb garden; its fragrant foliage was often tucked in the handkerchief drawer of her bureau.

And daisies *will* tell—if you can interpret what they are saying. The common oxeye daisy appears to grow almost everywhere. About all it needs is a sunny location. Knowing what you do now about the probable origin of such widespread plants, you might suspect that it too arrived with those groceries imported from Europe for pioneering livestock. This, indeed, was most likely the case. However, there seems to be no clear record as to when the first love-smitten youth in this country anxiously pulled those white rays from the edge of the yellow centers one by one—"She loves me . . . she loves me not . . . she loves me. . . ."

The daisy's scientific name, *Chrysanthemum leucanthemum*, tells that it must be a cousin of those powder-puff garden flowers. Unlike their wild relative, most cultivated 'mums have lost the central disc and have only the ray florets. If a lover solemnly pulled out every one of the scores of petals, it would give his beloved plenty of time to change her mind.

The common name of the daisy fleabane hints at its ancestry; it is the bane, or nemesis, of fleas. And not just fleas, but almost any insect. Pioneers hung dried bunches of fleabane inside their homes to ward off small unwanted visitors. I can remember my grandmother gathering this knee-high plant to furnish fragrant, flea-free lodging for the dog—especially when Brownie had her puppies.

Daisy fleabane, or *Erigeron annuus*, as the botanist knows it, is not a true daisy. However, it is closely related, as you would suspect on seeing those half-inch, hundred-rayed daisy-like flowers. Once it grew along river meadows, lake shores and similar breaks in the early woodland. Now it is often a debonair, sophisticated town dweller.

One more daisy-that-isn't: "stinkin' daisy," as we kids used to call it. *Anthemis cotula* may have come over from Europe in the same fashion as the oxeye daisy. Often just a few inches tall, the little plant looks like a tiny daisy as it lines the early summer roadsides from open country to about the region of the first traffic light. But if you rub its finely dissected leaves you'll probably never have to be told its name again. Mayweed, as it's known in polite society, has a terrible smell.

On the last day of school a group of boys in my home town picked a huge bunch of mayweed and put it on the teacher's desk for a bouquet. At least, that's how I think it went. For some reason I had a terrific headache that day and things were a little hazy.

Several other plants that look like the mayweed are easier to take. Known as chamomiles, they provide a more friendly atmosphere. Talking animals and children in fairy tales used to drink chamomile tea. So, most likely, did your grandmother. And so, for that matter, do numbers of people today who appreciate variety in their cup. You can buy dried chamomile at the local health store, or you can gather its fruit-scented leaves free with the help of a guidebook to weeds and flowers.

Smelling and looking like sweet chamomile but bearing a tiny rayless globular yellow flower is the pineapple weed, *Matricaria matricarioides*. Usually only a few inches high even if the lawnmower leaves it alone, pineapple weed grows along the edge of sidewalks and in the centers of driveways. You'll find it in almost any town of the northeast quarter of the United States and adjacent southern Canada. Its somewhat taller relative tansy (*Tanacetum vulgare*) has leaves that look as if they would be at home on a fern. Tansy's pill-shaped yellow flower looks like a daisy after someone has pulled off all the rays. Both these composites were valued for their sweet smell and were brought over from the old country for those early herb gardens.

I like the story of the orange hawkweed, *Hieracium aurantiacum*. With its four or five flowers resembling small orange dandelions at the top of a single stalk a foot high or more, the hawkweed was a colorful addition to the weeds in those early pastures. When its blossoms closed they looked like a brush dipped in artist's colors, so the plant also became known as "paintbrush." However, its coarse-haired leaves and stems irritated the mouths of livestock and caused them to reject the hay. So the farmer, ruefully surveying his inedible fields, added his own colorful epithet: "*devil's* paintbrush."

Today the imported devil's paintbrush aids our native yellow hawkweeds in outdoor decoration. There it is often joined by scores of other composite cousins: more than a dozen species of goldenrods, for instance, and an equal number of asters. Goldenrod flowers often grow in spires, or gracefully nodding stems, composed of dozens of tiny yellow heads. Asters are in clusters of blue, pink or white, usually with yellow centers. Each aster head bears many radiating petallike rays; hence its common and scientific name *Aster*—"star." Goldenrod's scientific name, *Solidago*, by the way, means "to make solid (whole)"—alluding to the old belief in the healing properties of its juice in a compress on a wounded part.

While you may wonder about goldenrod as a cure-all, chances are you have accepted another reputed property without blinking—its supposed ability to cause hay fever. But you might as well accuse the trees in the park or the neighbor's cat as to lay the blame for all that misery on the goldenrod. Its pollen is heavy, often moist and clustered, and more suited for clinging to the bodies of bees and butterflies than blowing away on the breeze. The true culprit is that inconspicuous green-flowered plant that we have already met—ragweed, which blooms at the same time. Strewn by the wind, ragweed pollen quietly assails your sinuses, while goldenrod gets the credit.

The yellows and pinks of goldenrod and aster are often joined by those of another plant family: the yellow evening primrose (*Cenothera biennis*) and its pink-flowered cousin the fireweed (*Epilobium angustifolium*). Both may be as tall as a person, with a central spike bearing long, slender leaves and four-petaled flowers. Evening primrose is named for its late-afternoon blooms, while fireweed is often the first bit of color on fire-blackened ground.

Another splash of color in the grimmest wasteland may be provided by butter-and-eggs (*Linaria vulgaris*). This foot-high plant, whose common name describes its color, looks like little snapdragons on a stalk. A tall relative, the common mullein, also belongs to the snapdragon family. Mullein bears a spike of yellow flowers that may reach six feet in height. Its foliage looks as if it were cut out of a fuzzy blanket, somehow matching its thick-tongued scientific name, *Verbascum thapsus*. If you cannot lisp that Latin term, just call mullein by its descriptive common nickname, flannel leaf.

Often standing with the mullein, but scarcely half as tall, are the white campions (*Silene* species) whose five petals grow from a swollen base. In some species, the base is almost like a tiny hollow ball. Their miniature relatives, the chickweeds, poke up among the grass blades of even the most respectable lawns, complete with little opposite-branching leaves and deep-notched white flowers.

More white is provided by the wild carrot, or Queen Anne's lace (*Daucus carota*). Their lacy flat clusters of tiny white blossoms often bear a central unopened bud of deep red—the drop of blood where Queen Anne pricked her finger with a needle in making the lace.

The common milkweed (*Asclepias syriaca*) is a fascinating plant. The stocky stem with the oval, opposite leaves and milky juice gets along just fine with old tires and bottles and discarded furniture. Beyond a place to send down a few roots all it seems to need is plenty of sunshine to help develop its rounded clusters of pinkish flowers.

And unusual flowers they are, too, with tiny slits into which the foot of an incautious bee may slide. Yanking its foot free, the struggling bee also pulls out a couple of little pollen sacks that cling to its leg like tiny saddlebags. The bags, drying in the air, may burst and pollinate the next blossom. Smaller insects, caught in the flowers, may stay there until they die; or, struggling enough, they may leave an imprisoned leg behind. Often, if you look closely at a milkweed blossom, you can see the legs or bodies of its little captives.

The pollinated blossom develops into a pointed capsule about the size of your thumb. The capsule splits along one edge when ripe, releasing scores of flattened little seed-parachutes, a few with every gust of wind.

One time a group of us took a field trip on Long Island. A glint in the sunshine caught our eyes. Some glittering object darted about at tremendous speed high in the heavens. A flying saucer? UFO? Visitor from another planet?

While we puzzled, the unknown object was joined by another. Now there were two. And then, when a sudden gust shook a milkweed near where we were standing, we understood. Those space capsules were the aerial seeds of the plant, wafted upward into the clear sky. Mistaking small size for great height, we thought we were seeing something large and distant, whereas it was really tiny and close. The "great speed," of course, when condensed down to size, was just the little balloonists changing direction with the eddying air currents. And here we thought we had a squadron of flying saucers for sure!

Unusual flowers, too, are found on many members of the buckwheat family. The individual flowers are inconspicuous and look like reddish-green chaff on the tall spikes that bear them. They hardly look like flowers at all. The tall spikes become seedstalks and may remain from one year to the next. Thus, you can spot the common dock (*Rumex obtusifolius*), whose huge broad leaves are shaped like an elongated heart. Its relative the curly dock (*R. crispus*) has more slender, crinkled leaves. Their little cousin *Rumex acetosella,* or sheep sorrel, has leaves only an inch or two long and shaped like an arrowhead. Any of these three species will settle in the seedier part of town, or in a formal flower bed when nobody is looking.

Often you find the red and green of the docks and sorrels mixed in with all those other colors—the gold of that ubiquitous dandelion; the orange of hawkweed and wasteland lilies; the blues, pinks, purples and whites of all the plants we have met, and dozens more.

Anne Ophelia Dowden, whose wonderful illustrations grace her book *Wild Green Things in the City* (Crowell, 1972), has counted ninety separate species of such plants in New York

Lambsquarters

City, growing untended but not always unappreciated, "in the cluttered 'gardens' of their own making." Sixty species have been found in Denver, and more than 130 in Los Angeles. And in between these cities, along thousands of miles of street and road and superhighway, stretch the ranks of these participants in what has been called "the world's greatest flower show."

One final plant for our list: that pioneer among pioneers, lamb's-quarters, or goosefoot (*Chenopodium album*). Turn over some soil almost anywhere and let it grow to what it will. Chances are that lamb's-quarters will be the first to sprout on the new surface. Its little black seeds must be gifted with eternal life; how else can you explain those seedlings that sprout up so quickly when the sod of an elderly lawn is disturbed, or when the soil is exposed where a building once stood? The seeds must have been buried there for decades, waiting for just the right conditions.

So far I have not said much about edible plants, because a mistake might lose me a lot of readers. Here, however, is an exception. You can spot lamb's-quarters easily. It's a worthwhile plant to know. The Amerindians and settlers relished the nutlike flavor of its seeds. So do today's natural-food fans. Its foliage is every bit as tasty as any greens you'll buy in the market, and even better than many.

Look for lamb's-quarters almost any place where new soil has been exposed. Unable to stand competition, it seldom exists more than a couple of summers, or until other plants move in. Its light-green leaves, when mature, are shaped like an elongated diamond, with a few blunt projections on the margin. Thus the name "goosefoot"—like a webbed foot with toes sticking out. The undersides of the leaves and the tiny new growth and developing buds are whitish and mealy in texture.

As the plant gets older, traces of red may be found on its stem and leaves. Its tiny greenish flowers are borne in clusters near the tip and upper part of the stem. Such flowers and foliage are too tough to eat, but once you are sure of your plant you can gather the younger stems and leaves. Cook them just like any good garden greens. Drain well; add butter and salt. Delicious!

One summer we served a fresh batch of pigweed (as lamb's-quarters is known locally) to our friends George and Ruth Strickholm. Afraid that they might balk if they knew its true identity, we dubbed it "Green Mountain Spinach." However, they were enthusiastic about it and had us point out the weed in the wild. I showed them where I had picked it—around a few boards left after a pile of lumber had been cleared away.

The next summer when we went to visit them, they took us out to their garden. "We liked your 'spinach' so much," George said, "that we found some of our own and saved it for seed."

At this point Ruth took up the conversation. "And there you are," she said triumphantly indicating a couple of well-tended strips of weeds right down the middle of her garden, "two rows of Green Mountain Spinach."

So, you see, it's all in your viewpoint. A weed is merely a plant out of place. When it is in its place it may be welcome, indeed.

Tomatoes .89#
Large Size Grapefruit 3/1.00
Georgia Peaches .69#
SPECIAL! Mushrooms 1.19#
1.19#
.89#
3/1.00
.69#

3·Mushrooms in the Metropolis

I'M SURE THERE IS NO CONNECTION, but I wish I knew what happened. Some day, perhaps, I'll find out. There is an ancient mushroom book in my collection that was begun by one author and finished by another. Author Number One tells of the joys of mushrooms and gives a number of recipes for their preparation. Then, without explanation, the book is completed by Author Number Two.

As I say, there probably is no connection. But it makes you wonder. Mushrooms can be tricky, sometimes. You cannot be too careful.

Most people leave all mushrooms where they find them. They would rather not take chances. The few poisonous kinds of mushrooms have given a bad name to the whole lot. And that, really, is unfortunate. There are only a handful that are unkind enough to your innards even to be called unwholesome. Some of these merely come back up after you've downed them—a startling development, but hardly fatal. The real villains, those that could do you in, number about half a dozen out of a couple hundred species that might be found on our North American continent.

Not all of these, of course, share your surroundings if you live in the suburbs. Even fewer really get downtown. Yet I once saw a group of youngsters having a mushroom fight in a park near the center of Sharon, Pennsylvania; they were using good, edible *Agaricus* mushrooms for ammunition. And on Boston Common there are several crops of old-stump mushrooms each year.

The Boston mushrooms do not last any longer than those in the Battle of Sharon either. However, they disappear for a different reason. Today's enlightened generation, with its interest in natural foods, easily recognizes them for the delicious morsels they are. Barely do they poke aboveground than they're harvested for somebody's dinner.

Yes, it is possible to tell the good from the bad. What's more, you can save a few cents in the process, right in the shadow of the supermarket. There are several mushrooms that are completely wholesome and almost foolproof as to identification. Even so, however, since I cannot be right there with you, perhaps I should put in a little disclaimer saying my responsibility would be limited to the purchase price of this book. Or something to that effect.

I remember one time when I was driving through Pittsfield, Massachusetts, with the family. We were going to visit my parents in Connecticut for the weekend. Tom, who was about ten years old and a good outdoorsman, yelped at me to stop when he spotted some mushrooms on a lawn. Hastily pulling over to the curb to the accompaniment of startled glances from other drivers around me, I got out for a better look. The mushrooms were there by the score: perhaps twenty pounds of a good, delicious kind known as the shaggymane.

Going to the door of the house, I knocked. A woman opened the door part way. "Yes?"

"I'm interested in mushrooms," I began, "and wonder if you have any plans for those that are growing on your lawn—"

She looked out beyond me. "You mean those things out there—those toadstools? The only plans I have is to get rid of the whole batch."

"Then you wouldn't mind if I picked a few and took them along?"

Now she guessed what I had in mind. "Oh, no you don't! I'm not going to have any lawsuit on my hands!"

She was in no mood to argue, so I made what I hoped was a graceful exit. As we drove away we could see several faces at the window. Obviously the whole family considered that I was daft.

On the way back through the town a couple of days later we slowed down to have another look at that forbidden fruit. But all we saw were little pieces all over the lawn. Even though it was mid-October and the grass had nearly quit growing, that jittery family was taking no chances. Getting out the power mower, they'd scrambled the whole works.

Shaggymane (*Coprinus comatus*) is actually one of the easiest mushrooms to identify. You can spot it on several points. First, it's almost always an autumn mushroom. Then, too, it seems to enjoy the company of people. When Peg and I lived on Long Island we often saw it on lawns as we drove in toward New York City. It may grow around dumps, too, but I've never found it far removed from where people are around and active nearly every day.

Another feature of the shaggymane is its striking appearance. Cylindrical, white, and as much as ten inches high, it is one of the tallest mushrooms. Sometimes it forms clusters so dense that they raise little patches of lawn upward as they grow. Instead of spreading out, umbrellawise, as do most mushrooms, shaggymane's cap at first remains closely cupped about the stem. The cap is ragged and sprinkled with tan-colored scales that give it a disheveled appearance; hence its common name.

When it is several days old the cap expands and dissolves into an inky-black fluid. By this time it's too mushy to eat, but the change in its appearance clinches your identification so you'll recognize it next time. It's sort of like the test for gold: you dip the hoped-for metal into a concoction of strong acids known as *aqua regia*. Then, if it disappears, it *was* gold.

Shaggymane has a couple of cousins, the inky cap (*Coprinus atramentarius*) and the glistening coprinus (C. *micaceus*). They both grow in clusters of many crowded, brownish, egg-shaped caps about the size of the last joint of your thumb. You'll often find them at the base of rotting trees, or even on a lawn where an old stump has been buried. They do not cause the death of the tree, but serve as a clean-up crew in reducing the wood to humus.

Like their large shaggy relative, the inky mushrooms dissolve into a black sludge when mature—thus hinting that, if you had been quick enough, you could have had a mushroom meal. Fortunately, the crop may be continuous for a week or more on a single stump. In addition, they may grow any time from May to November. Thus, if you miss one harvest, you may find another waiting somewhere else. With the shaggymane, about all you can do is remember the place and wait for next year.

By the way, don't dismiss the possibilities of wild mushrooms just because you are already familiar with the cultivated variety. This is like saying that you know what fruit tastes like because you ate an apple once. Each mushroom has its own flavor and texture. The commercial species can be delicious, yes—but not after languishing to the point of extinction in some supermarket bin. And if all you've had are a few of these tired old offerings, you are comparing yesterday's toast with today's homemade bread right out of the oven.

There are various ways to prepare mushrooms. You can eat them raw and unexpurgated, or boiled, or dried, or as *champignons au vin*, which is French for "dunked in wine for a week." A simple method is to fry them in a little butter and serve as you would onion rings or french fries.

If you have any leftovers, cut them into small pieces, put them in an airtight container and pop them into the freezer. Be sure to sauté or pan-fry first, however. Otherwise, when you exhume them later, all that remains upon thawing is a clutch of soggy mushrooms.

The cultivated mushroom, incidentally, is merely the civilized variety of the common lawn and pasture species, *Agaricus campestris.* It was this mushroom that furnished the ammunition for those gleeful kids on that park lawn. Together with its larger cousin the horse mushroom (*A. arvensis*), this common agaric, as it is sometimes called, is the trophy most often brought home for food.

Look for either species on any grassy area. Last July we visited Dick and Freda King in Raleigh, North Carolina. Dick teaches at North Carolina State University. It had rained several days in a row, and the usually well-tended lawns on the campus were so juicy that the maintenance crews had been forced to take a week off. This was just the opportunity the mushrooms had been waiting for: they dotted the lawns in several places. Their domed white caps, poking up through the lengthening grass, looked as if some golfer had whacked out a bucket of balls.

With the exception of size, these two *Agaricus* mushrooms resemble each other. The smaller *campestris,* when grown, has a cap about the size of half an orange. The cap at first has a thin veil on its lower side. Initially the veil is unbroken, so the entire cap looks like a solid hemisphere. Then, tearing away in shreds until only a flimsy ring is left on the stem, the veil discloses hundreds of thin pinkish gills on the underside of the cap. The gills darken until they are brown. The cap often expands, the better to expose the millions of microscopic spores borne on the gills.

Cap, veil and pinkish gills are also borne by the larger horse mushroom. At one time it lived in well-used pastures; hence its common name. Now, lacking its equine companions, it has traded the richness of animal manure for that of commercial fertilizers and buried organic matter on lawns, golf courses and ball fields. A herd of horse mushrooms is an impressive sight, with occasional specimens fully the size of a dinner plate. And, like its smaller relative, this mushroom gets things done suddenly. It may go through the entire process from that juvenile "button" stage with unbroken veil to the brownish expanded adult in just a few days.

Unfortunately, a couple of "toadstools"—a common name for any poisonous mushroom—resemble these two kinds of *Agaricus*. Belonging to the genus *Amanita*, they bear such charming names as death angel, destroying angel, and widow maker.

There are several species of *Amanita*. Like their more respectable second cousins they may be found on lawns or golf courses, but they are more often seen at the edges of woods or in park groves. They are large, handsome, and—according to those who have made the mistake and lived to tell about it—simply delicious. So you cannot tell a good fungus from a bad merely by the taste.

Nor, by the way, can you make the distinction according to the old belief that a silver spoon put in with bad mushrooms will soon turn black. Not all "toadstools" are this obliging. And some wholesome kinds, unfamiliar with the rules, will give a spoon a beautiful tarnish. Besides, how soon is "soon"? What if you put the spoon in the pot and then didn't wait long enough?

No. The best way is to learn the difference. There are several distinctive danger signs. While the edible *Agaricus* has a veil that stretches beneath its cap when young, a more extensive membrane covers the whole mushroom like a shroud in the developing button stage of *Amanita*. As the plant grows it rips the veil away, leaving some of it around the swollen base so that it resembles a sac. This sac is sometimes called the "death cup."

More of the veil may remain on the upper surface of the cap of *Amanita* as scales or patches. In some species the cap is white; in others it is orange or yellowish. There's a ring around the stem, too, just as in *Agaricus*. However, the gills are white or at best yellowish, instead of the pink-to-brown progression in the edible lawn and horse mushrooms.

Sound complicated? Not really. If you see white gills, a "death cup" and a swollen base on a mushroom, better scrap your dinner plans. Lack of these warning signals, on the other hand, doesn't necessarily mean to heat up the skillet. It just signifies, if you'll pardon the double play on words, that you probably are in the right ball park. Which grassy place, you see, is often a productive spot for mushrooms, especially after a rainy season.

By now you may have decided to get your mushrooms at a safe grocery store. This is probably the wisest course to follow, at that—unless you take as a guide more than these few paragraphs. However, you can still enjoy mushrooms on less intimate terms. They can be interesting whether you plan to invite them to dinner or not. In case you want to get acquainted, some of them will meet you halfway. Really.

Mushroom spores, it seems, are everywhere. Or just about, at any rate. A single medium-sized specimen may release several million spores per day during the week or so of its existence. These microscopic bits of life float on every air current, gradually sifting down like a layer of invisible dust. You probably are breathing them now as you read these words.

With no power of choice, many spores fall on inhospitable ground: the pavement, a roof, the surface of a lake. Even those that land in a lawn or garden must come to rest where they can obtain ready nourishment. Unlike a seed, they contain no food of their own. The rare one-in-a-million, however, finds more friendly lodging on a pile of decaying leaves, say, or a piece of wood in contact with soil or moisture.

This may be all the encouragement a mushroom spore needs. Buried right on its food, perhaps, as a tractor smoothes debris into a building site, or subsiding into the ground with rotting leaves, the spore germinates and forms a skein of whitish threads. You probably have seen these threads—a mass of them is called a *mycelium*—beneath the bark of a decaying tree, or between boards in a forgotten lumber pile.

The mycelium may grow for months or even years, hidden there in the dark. Then, in its own good time, it sends forth a mushroom. Or a dozen or more.

The direction of growth of that mycelium is limited by the availability of its food—along the length of a buried plank, for instance, or within a maze of long-dead roots. Sometimes, however, there may be enough organic matter—say a weed bed that was bulldozed to bits—to allow it to grow from a central point in all directions. Spreading outward, it produces a radial pattern, like a ghostly wheel beneath the soil. Then, in its bid for a return to the upper world, it sends up a mushroom at the end of each "spoke" of the wheel. The result is a circle, sometimes many yards in diameter, that may contain several dozen fungi. Known as a "fairy ring," it can sprout up overnight. Then, the next morning, you stand perplexed and wonder how on earth *that* ever got there.

With the essentials of life satisfied—food, moisture, and proper temperature—the mycelium may get along with no soil at all. Some friends of ours had a leak in the roof. With every hard rain the water seeped in, forming a spot on the ceiling. The landlord promised to fix it, but it was weeks before the workmen came to do the job.

The crew patched the roof, all right but didn't replace the rotten timbers of the wall. When Peg and I visited our friends last spring, there was the end result of it all, recorded right on the ceiling. A little cluster of about ten white mushrooms nestled in the corner over the television.

"They're the second batch," Linda Sherman informed us. "The first time we had only four of them."

Were they concerned about this addition to their living room? "Nope," said Hank Sherman. "They're a great conversation piece. And besides, we can't wait to see how many there'll be in the *third* crop."

With increasing use of rough wood slabs, complete with bark, as siding for a porch or dormer, similar decorations may take place in other homes. However, they most likely will be on the outside. Besides, they will last only until the siding dries out. The reason the Shermans got a rerun, there in television corner, was that the hidden wood in the wall still held enough moisture.

Rough wood slabs, sliced away from the main log, may carry the fungus with them, or they may have picked it up en route from lumber yard to your renovation project. It is hard to tell. However, one point is certain: if you see fungi growing on the side of a tree trunk, it's too late to worry about saving that tree. The mushroom—or conk, as the lumberman calls it—develops only after the mycelium is well aged. In the process it has pervaded much of the wood. So, better start a second tree, while you have time, to replace that first one when it conks out.

One of the easiest mushrooms to identify grows as an embellishment on a decrepit tree. This is the oyster mushroom, *Pleurotus*. It forms clusters at almost any point on the tree, from the base of the trunk to a dead limb high in the air. Rank on rank, like shelves placed one above the other, this mushroom resembles oysters growing on a marine piling; hence its name.

There are two common species. One grows on elms, and is

known scientifically as *Pleurotus ulmarius*. The other grows on many trees, and bears the botanical name of *Pleurotus sapidus*. If you recall that "sapid" means tasty or delectable, you can guess that at least one scientist liked to eat.

Actually, it doesn't matter which species of oyster mushroom you have. To our way of thinking, *both* are sapid—and then some.

Besides their unusual habit of growth, oyster mushrooms have an individual shape all their own. Instead of having a cap and a stem in traditional mushroom fashion, they are practically stemless. Attached to each other or to the tree by the edge of the cap, they are like white, tan or buffy inverted saucers ranging in diameter from one to six inches or more. The light-colored gills fan out from the point of attachment much like the rays of the scallop trademark of the Shell Oil Company.

You may find oyster mushrooms at any time from June to December. The winter specimens are holdovers from the fall crop. Even when frozen solid they are still worth gathering: tough, but tasty.

Although these mushrooms grow on dead wood, they may be innocent of the killing of the tree itself. Like almost all living things they are opportunists, taking the breaks as they come along. And a "break" may be just that: a fractured branch, for instance, or the attack of disease. As progressive parts of the tree die, the mycelium advances, a camp follower cleaning up after the battle.

With the loss of millions of elms to Dutch elm disease, these secondary saprophytes—fungi that feed on dead plant material—have been having a field day. A formerly tree-shaded boulevard may now be lined with whitened skeletons of elm. The dead trees were overwhelmed by the unseen disease organism, but those highly visible oyster mushrooms get all the blame.

Mushrooms in the Metropolis

Several years ago an ice storm crippled much of the Northeast. Although the precipitation fell as rain, it landed on a world chilled well below the freezing temperature. Thus, the rain froze as it hit, building up a coating of ice on roads and wires and bushes.

Driving was impossible; even if you could somehow negotiate the icy street, there was no place to go. Wires were down; trees drooped so low as to strike the car as you drove. Huge limbs, unable to bear the weight of their own encrusted branches, split off and crashed to earth. Many trees were completely destroyed. Each limb tore away at the fork, leaving nothing but the main trunk standing in the center of a great brush pile.

Highway and utility line crews worked heroically. They cleaned up the mess so that essential traffic could flow and services could be restored. But thousands of trees in less critical locations were not so favored. Today, nearly a decade after that storm, you can still see broken limbs hung up in trees. Many of them now bear their own crop of oyster mushrooms. I saw one such tree at the edge of Elizabeth Park in Hartford, holding aloft enough food for a banquet.

Oyster mushrooms, by the way, look like the familiar shelf mushrooms, or bracket fungi, that also grow on dead trees. Bracket fungi come in a range of sizes. The largest would scarcely fit on a card table. The smallest are tiny scales only a fraction of the size of your fingernail. Some are black, some are white. One species looks as if it were freshly coated with varnish. Others may have rich purples, buff, deep chocolate brown in concentric bands.

You can spot the difference between oyster mushrooms and bracket fungi by a glance at the underside. Instead of a series of gills, the bracket fungi bear thousands of tiny pores. These pores are really the ends of miniature tubes through which the spores are released.

That porous undersurface is often immaculately white in the living fungus. Some species have a yellow tint, or green, or even maroon. Scratch them with a stick or toothpick and they'll often turn brown at the point of injury. One way to get a lasting and attractive souvenir of an afternoon's walk is to pick a bracket fungus from some spot where nobody will miss it, and then inscribe it with the appropriate wording. Or draw a picture; once dried, your work of art will almost last forever. It makes an interesting addition to your desk or mantel or kitchen table.

Don't be concerned about its edibility, by the way. As far as I have ever heard, no true bracket fungus is poisonous. But even if it were harmful, you still needn't worry. A bona fide bracket fungus, cooked or uncooked, is just about unchewable. As my grandmother would say, it's about as tender as a boiled owl.

There is another way to gain a souvenir from a meeting with a mushroom. This is in the making of a spore print. Simple to create, a spore print can be an item of surprising beauty and complexity. All you need is any kind of gilled mushroom, a sheet of paper, some stiff cardboard, and a bowl large enough to fit over the mushroom cap. Secure the paper to the sheet of cardboard so that you can lift it later without flexing it. Place paper and cardboard on a flat surface away from drafts. Put the mushroom cap, gills down, on the paper and invert the bowl over it. The bowl will create a calm atmosphere around the cap so the millions of spores will fall without blowing around.

Leave the bowl in place overnight; then carefully remove bowl and cap in the morning. The spores will have created a ghostly pattern of the mushroom gills on the paper. It's a surprisingly intricate pattern, and may range in color from off-white to lilac or purple or brown. For more dramatic effect, use black paper with the light-spored species; white paper with the dark ones.

Those tiny spores will smear with the first touch or breath of wind, so they must be "fixed" on the paper. This may be done by misting carefully with a hair spray, or by lightly puffing varnish on with an atomizer. Then, once rendered permanent, the design on the paper can be shellacked onto a wall plaque or merely hung as a decoration. And since you're seldom more than a few city blocks away from a mushroom of some description, the raw material for your own conversation piece is usually at hand.

One of my favorites is a conversation piece in itself, just as it grows. This is the startling *Lycoperdon giganteum*, the giant puffball. And it is, indeed, a giant among fungi; a single specimen may weigh as much as ten pounds.

There are two ways the giant puffball chooses to make its entrance into the world. Often it starts as a little white button there on the library lawn, say, or next to the town flagpole. The second day it's the size of an egg. The third day it looks as if somebody has lost a softball; the fourth it's like a white bowling ball—and so on, until it has reached full size. The whole process takes about a week.

The second method of putting in an appearance is for most of the small stages to take place underground. Then, when the burgeoning puffball can no longer remain hidden, it erupts from the soil almost overnight. If you're lucky enough to spot it as it is emerging, it looks as if a soup plate were pushing up from below.

If allowed to go its way unmolested, the giant puffball turns from a light tan to an increasingly dark brown. Its interior, at first moist and mealy-white, becomes yellow and then smoky in color. It is smoky in texture, too: the inner substance of a puffball is made almost completely of spores—millions upon millions of them. It has been estimated that a puffball one foot in diameter may contain seven trillion spores.

It's next to impossible to make a mistake in eating a puffball. Most books agree that none is poisonous. One, found on fallen logs in wooded groves, has a skin as tough as orange peel, and a jet black interior that hardly looks appetizing, but it too apparently is all right.

The thing is to be sure you have a puffball in the first place. If you plan to eat it, cut it right down the middle, just to be sure. If it's homogeneous and granular throughout, you have a meal. If it shows any structure—tiny stem, little gills, or a developing cap—you have some mushroom in the "button" stage. Better let it alone; there's not much certainty what it may be, but it's definitely not a puffball.

The giant puffball is most obliging about providing your meal, by the way. If you like your mushrooms fresh, just slice off what you need and allow the rest to stay right where it is. It will continue to grow, apparently unperturbed by the loss. Then, if you wish a second sitting of the same mushroom, return and slice off some more.

One time, when I was doing some graduate work at the University of Connecticut, I found a giant puffball growing on the lawn near the administration building. It looked to be only half grown, and it seemed a shame to yank it up by the roots, so I cut about a third of it off for supper. Then, knowing that it probably would get kicked to bits if some playful students found it, I scraped up a pile of leaves from a nearby corner of the building and arranged them over the big mushroom. Trying to make the pile look as haphazard as possible, I sprinkled the leaves casually and sauntered away.

Peg was delighted with our good fortune. The puffball would provide a welcome change from the "economical-but-nourishing" foods we had been getting along with while I struggled to get that advanced degree. We sliced the chunk into half-inch slabs, cut them into cubes, fried them in oleomargarine, and had a gourmet banquet on a grad-student budget.

After a few days I went back for another chunk of

mushroom. By now, I figured, it must be fully grown and more than ready to part with another segment of its anatomy. Carefully digging through the pile of leaves, I uncovered my giant puffball.

Well, almost giant. Now it had *two* cuts: mine, and another one. Apparently someone had seen my little performance of a few days earlier. Investigating the pile of leaves, whoever-it-was had also taken a slab. And stuck into the unfortunate puffball was a sheet ripped out of a small notebook and pinned in place with a stick. "Thanks," it said. "Your turn again."

Giant puffballs are autumn mushrooms, just like the shaggymane. There are smaller puffballs at other seasons, however, just as there are other fungi. In fact, there's hardly any time you'll not find at least some of these interesting specimens of plant life.

Hardly any place, either. On a recent trip to the Midwest, for instance, we were guests of Mr. and Mrs. Bill Allen of Minneapolis. It had been a rainy June and the weather was cool—ideal conditions for mushrooms. A couple of days before we arrived a few strange mushrooms had put in an appearance on their side lawn. They considered them uneasily, wondering whether to wait to show them to us or to destroy them before some neighbor's kid ended up in the hospital.

Finally they decided to allow them to stay. However, Marge would take no chances. She put a wire basket over the suspicious fungi and weighted it down with a cement block. The first thing they did after we brought in our suitcases was to take us out for an official viewing.

It was gratifying to know they had taken such pains so that we could look at a couple of mushrooms. But it was a bit upsetting too. I had the sneaky feeling that Bill and Marge thought of us as mushroom experts, instead of merely the hobbyists we were. What if we failed?

One look, however, was all we needed. Beneath that wire

basket were some of the most sought-after delicacies of the entire world of mushrooms: four large specimens of *Morchella esculenta,* the esculent and delightful morel.

Hardly believing our luck right here in the Minneapolis city limits, we pointed out the features of this much-prized mushroom. Nearly six inches high, each morel looked like a pointed sponge on a thick stalk. Marge decided that it looked more like a chunk of brown tripe on a stick—hardly an appetizing description. But then, morels are supposed to be exquisite to the taste, not the eye.

After we had photographed the morels, I broke one of them in half. The hollowness of these mushrooms always surprises me; they're nothing but a shell from tip of cap to base of stem. "But they're so good that people even put them in salads," I said. "Raw."

Marge and Bill echoed as one voice: "*Raw?*"

Without thinking, I popped a piece into my mouth. "Raw."

They watched me, impressed. When I swallowed, they swallowed too. Actually, I prefer to wait until my mushrooms are cooked—even the esculent morel. But they are good in salads, often retaining their texture after the lettuce has wilted.

When our hosts realized that I wasn't going to drop, we looked around for more. There was a small one under a lilac bush and one just over the line, by a neighbor's hedge. We got permission to get the one near the hedge and took them all into the house.

That evening Marge defrosted four jiffy steaks that she had in the freezer. We broke the morels into half-inch pieces, browned them well in butter, and spread them over the little steaks. There wasn't a better dinner served in Minneapolis that night.

I wish I could describe the taste of the morel, but tastes like that are hard to put into words. Toasted coconut comes to mind, perhaps, but not exactly. Peg cannot stand coconut, and she's as fond of morels as I am. The cooked texture and possibly the flavor as well are something like a sweet omelet. But that's not right, either. People wouldn't practically take leave of their senses for a sweet omelet. And if you don't think morel eaters are zany, just try to find out exactly where somebody picked his latest morel meal. You might as well ask a fisherman where he caught that Big One.

At any rate, we made a couple of converts in a single meal. You too might become converted, if the chance afforded. Morels are not really hard to find; it's just that they do not always come up twice in the same place. Two conditions seem to favor their growth: ground where an elm tree has stood in the past, and an area where there has been a fire. So, I suppose, the ideal place to look for them would be where somebody burned some elm wood.

But people do make mistakes, even on a unique mushroom like a morel. There's *Phallus impudicus*, for instance—a skinny, vile-smelling, greenish-capped apparition known as a stinkhorn. I suppose you might think it was a morel if you were color-blind and suffering from sinus trouble. Another species of doubtful edibility is brown and shapeless, like a lump of dough. *Gyromitra brunnea*, as it is called, has a stem and cap that are solid; not hollow as in the morel. Its cap lacks the morel's honeycombed appearance, and the stem is irregular in cross section, not oval or cylindrical like the morel.

Still, if you do positively identify a group of morels and feel a little squeamish, better not take chances. Pack them carefully and ship them off to me. Airmail, prepaid. I might let you know the results of my experiments in a couple of weeks. After all, you cannot be too careful.

4·Room for One Million More

TWO LONG ANTENNAE wave at you questioningly. Two compound eyes scrutinize your every move. Six legs are poised, ready for instant flight. Are you friend or foe?

Probably foe. That little creature, there in front of you, seems to have few friends. It would never win a popularity contest. Nor, for that matter, a beauty competition. But in a vote to determine the one most likely to succeed the overwhelming favorite would have to be—brace yourself—the cockroach.

A humid little hovel down there among the foundations and water pipes may seem an unlikely place from which to come out on top, but the cockroach has done just that. Nor is it merely a fly-by-night; one of nature's trials that may soon prove to be an error. It has had ample time to work out schemes for beating the odds—some 350 million years, in fact. And today it is one of the world's most efficient scroungers of food and shelter that ever existed.

It's hard to single out any one feature that gives the cockroach such an edge over the competition. Other creatures can run faster, defend themselves better, produce more babies. And, heaven knows, hardly any other creature is singled out as the target for as many sprays and traps and death-dealing bombs. It's just that the Blattidae—which is the scientist's term for the cockroach family, and a name that somehow seems fit—is a marvel at adjusting to adversity.

Consider the vital statistics of a cockroach for a moment. It has nearly a 1-1-1 figure; these could be inches or centimeters or even millimeters, depending on the species. It's scarcely our idea of an insect Venus, but such dimensions serve it well. Aided by a smooth, flattened body and six hard-striving legs, the cockroach can push its way into almost impossible situations. And if they do, indeed, turn out to be impossible, its watermelon-seed proportions allow it to back-pedal until it's free again.

That leathery body is a self-contained suit of armor. It sheds water, dirt, and droplets from sure-fire cockroach spray with ease. It can flatten out under a good swipe from a cat's paw or the blow of a flyswatter and spring right back to shape. Sometimes it even works if the cockroach is on its back. Those long legs, instead of merely waving in the air, flail furiously to propel their overturned owner along until some stroke of luck allows it to right itself.

Such extras can be found piecemeal in other insects, but the cockroach has them all. In addition, its cosmopolitan food habits allow it to exist on anything from an extinct mouse to the glue in your stamp collection. Indeed, it can live nearly three months on nothing at all.

Yes, the cockroach is in a fair way to succeed long after many of its neighbors have tried and failed. It had been on earth about 180 million years before the dinosaurs arrived. It watched them die out a hundred million years later—doubtless saying, if it could, that it knew they wouldn't last.

Fossil evidence points out that cockroaches shared their caves with the first people, too. And they have been sharing ever since. It scarcely matters if the "cave" is perched ten stories in the air or speeding along on rails or afloat on the ocean; the durable cockroach can find something to its liking almost anywhere. Nor is it necessarily relegated to the pipes and drains and similar nether portions of its twentieth-century habitat. While the cockroach prefers moisture, it is also attracted by warmth. Thus the back side of a refrigerator may be an ideal spot, complete with the friendliness of a warm electric motor and the hospitality of a few crumbs. A television set is nice and cozy, too. So is an electric clock.

But before you abdicate and leave the premises to the cockroaches, let me add a couple of more points. In spite of the sleazy nature of its surroundings, the cockroach itself is immaculately clean. It spends hours grooming itself like a cat. Foreign material adhering to the spines and the few hairs of its body is carefully licked away. And, in spite of long and intimate association with people, it has yet to be proven as a necessary host for a single human disease. So, you see, a cockroach may live in dirt and filth, but the dirt and filth are ours. It was doing fine among the coal-age mosses and stone-age mastodons before we moderns came along and simplified things.

Another reason the cockroach does so well is its thoughtful family life. Many insects lay their eggs and leave them to their fate, but not the cockroach. The female deposits some three dozen of her eggs in a tough-skinned little purse, or *ootheca.* She attaches this capsule to the end of her abdomen and totes it around until it hatches. In this way the youngsters, or nymphs, are never far from the good life as enjoyed by their parents. Some species haul the ootheca to the tastiest spot they can find and then attach it right in the middle of breakfast. Still others shortcut the whole process, hatching the youngsters inside their bodies.

In any event, the nymphs are born on the run, so to speak. They look like miniatures of their parents and are ready to travel at once.

I remember taking a swat at a female German cockroach (*Blattella germanica*) when Peg and I lived in a one-room apartment during the war. The swat was right on target, and the female was no more. The egg case attached to her tail section, however, ruptured with the blow. About two dozen brand-new youngsters, born in a split second, lit out for cover. Their creamy-white bodies wavered as they desperately forced tiny new legs, still soft, to their unaccustomed task. With such a will to live, it's no wonder there always seem to be more cockroaches.

As you know, this book occasionally gives a few thoughts on the care and feeding of some of those plants and animals that share our streets and parks and old lots. Here are your instructions for the cockroach:

1. Leave plenty of food around. Don't put it in sealed jars or packages. Scatter leftovers well, too, especially old beer cans and bottles. They love the stuff, but be careful. Nothing in their past billion generations has taught cockroaches to cope with a half-empty container of beer. Somewhat unsettled by the heady brew, they lose their footing by the dozens. A normal cockroach can swim very well, but when inebriated it may end up deep in its cups—literally.

2. Keep potential roachariums dank and dark. Musty cloths hung on the S-trap under the sink will help. So will a leaky pipe fitting. And don't let any cleansers or electric lights come near the place.

3. Shun such tactics as scattering boric acid or rotenone powders where the cockroaches might scamper through them. Although the powders are practically harmless to children or pets, they are manifestly unfair to cockroaches. These fastidious creatures, in their daily cleansings, may swallow any

powder that clings to their feet or bodies and acquire a fatal case of dyspepsia.

One last thought about roaches. There are a couple of thousand species, more or less; nobody knows the number for sure, as they are so secretive. The three most likely to succeed in our land of opportunity are the aforementioned German cockroach, the Oriental cockroach (*Blatta orientalis*) and the American cockroach (*Periplaneta americana*). Such names sound as if they enjoyed distinct nationalities, but this is probably a matter of passing the buck. It is sort of like the mother who says to her husband, "George! Speak to *your* son!"

Even if the German cockroach was originally German—which I doubt—it has had plenty of chances to go international. Airport security measures and sharp-eyed customs agents mean little to a critter that can stow away in a luggage seam. In fact, the German cockroach enjoys another title in the area of New York City: the Croton bug. It seems that it flourishes along the great pipes of the Croton Aqueduct water system. And, if you spot the same creature in Berlin, say, or Frankfurt, you'll discover that you've got the name all wrong. It's the Russian cockroach.

A cockroach relative that enjoys a much better reception on the part of its human neighbors is the praying mantis. Originally confined to warmer climes, it has been steadily marching northward through the years. When I was a boy in Connecticut a mantis was something seen only in books. But by the time I was in college it had made it at least as far as my home state. The first mantis I ever saw had fluttered down right in the middle of Hartford. The three-inch insect held its ground, there on State Street, front legs flexed to battle the whole city, if necessary. Amused pedestrians stopped in mid-crosswalk, halting traffic in four directions. At last one spectator managed to persuade the pugnacious creature to climb on a piece of cardboard. The man disappeared into the crowd and the capital city of Connecticut went back to business as usual.

The praying mantis is like that. Fear seems never to enter what passes for a brain behind that heart-shaped face with those great, solemn eyes. Poised on four of its six legs, it raises the front two in defiance or threat. Folded against each other like a jacknife, the two spiny segments of the front legs are ready to lash out at a fly, a finger or a foot—it doesn't seem to matter which. Able to turn its head in almost human fashion, it studies your every move.

Insects are its preferred food. Once clamped between those spiny front legs the hapless victims are consumed with the same leisurely dispatch we would use in eating an ear of corn. Since insects are readily found wherever a few plants get together, the mantis is liable to be found there too. And, as the popular human opinion seems to be that most of those insects are harmful, the mantis enjoys immunity wherever it appears because of its well-known appetite.

You can even set yourself up in the mantis business. Many garden-supply stores will furnish a handful of mantis egg cases, or oothecae, on receipt of your order. Looking like a piece of tan styrofoam about the size of a large marble, each case cradles a couple of hundred eggs. In due time the eggs hatch, and your lawn or patio or window box will soon be free, the advertisement says, of harmful insects.

Sometimes it may work just that way, too. The ravenous little nymphs of *Stagmomantis carolina*, or any of its two dozen American cousins, fall to their task at once. If that "task" involves aphids or beetles or caterpillars, your money may have been well invested. On occasion, however, it reaps an unexpected—and uninvited—dividend. Also feeding on those plant pests may be other little predators: ladybugs, for instance, and lacewing flies and beneficial spiders. Scarcely

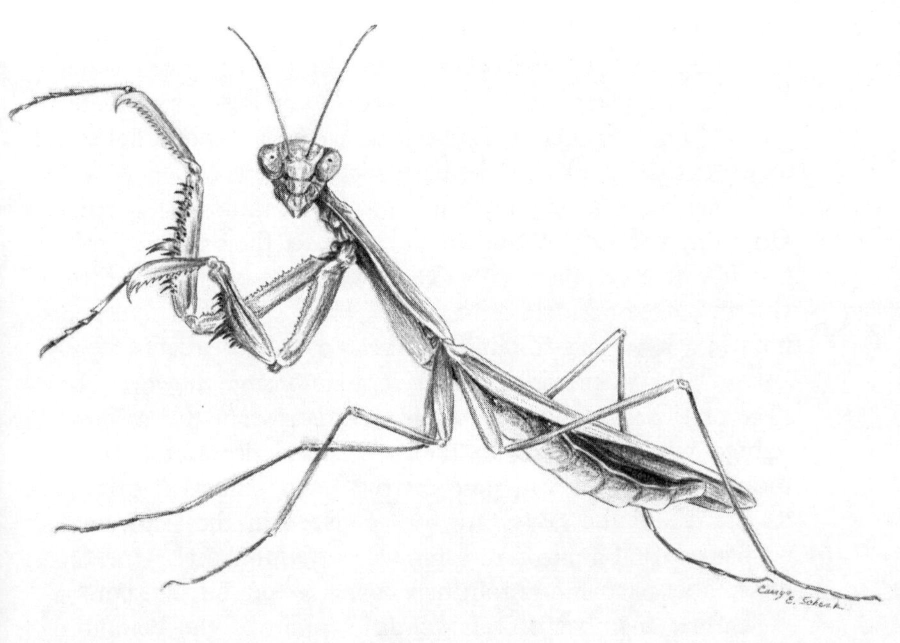

Praying Mantis

gifted with the power of discrimination, the mantids help themselves to nearly everything that moves, be it predator or prey. If the food supply doesn't keep pace with those fierce little appetites the mantids may even turn on each other. Or they set out to make their fortunes elsewhere.

Even without such tinkering with its natural balance, the mantis is a born adventurer. The female has no compunction as to where she leaves her egg cases. She bestows them on late summer weed stalks, the sides of buildings, or cement blocks lying in the grass. From there they may be taken up and carried for miles. A friend of mine who is fond of dried-flower bouquets created an arrangement that consisted of winter fruits and berries, rocks, driftwood—and two mantis egg cases. She discovered the nature of the egg cases when that pair of plant "galls" came to life in the warm room. There they launched what seemed to be a thousand baby mantises that ran all over the place like ants.

So a menage of mantises may not be an unmixed blessing. However, you usually find them singly, as they prefer a solitary life. In case you want to keep one, it's a fascinating little creature, needing little more than a large jar with a screened mouth, a few twigs to cling to, and a couple of insects daily.

Don't try to provide it with companionship, however. In spite of their keenness of vision, mantises seem to be shortsighted when it comes to their own kind. Forever hungry, the greater mantis will dine on the lesser—unless it relaxes its guard and the tables are turned. Even in the tender act of mating, that amazon of a female may throw a vise-grip on her smaller partner and routinely consume him on the spot.

Another member of this versatile family is the common cricket. It combines some of the features of cockroaches with those of the mantids and its grasshopper cousins. Hopping like a grasshopper, a cricket can also run and even fly as some cockroaches do. While it usually eats plant material, it's not above consuming an occasional neighbor, in the manner of a mantis.

Crickets spend their summers in the fields, but as autumn approaches they often seek the company of man and his buildings. *Acheta assimilis,* as the field cricket is known, makes its way into garages and cellars, workshops and greenhouses. Many a hotel, apartment house and school has its complement of crickets, settled among the basement steam pipes, cheerfully chirping the winter away. One species has deserted the outdoors entirely. It plies the oceans of the world in the holds of ships, and it sometimes disembarks with the passengers and accompanies them to their homes. Today it is the "cricket on the hearth," or *Acheta domesticus*—which, sensibly enough, means "house cricket."

Like the cockroach, this perky little critter has little difficulty in collecting a meal. A few crumbs will keep it for a week, an apple core for a month. It may also consume the egg cases of its cockroach cousins, plus a baby cockroach or injured adult when the chance affords.

Usually that mercurial, wingless insect known as the silverfish is too swift for a cricket, but the eggs and young are more easily managed. And since silverfish are regarded with dismay by librarians, who lose their paste, and laundry workers, who lose their starch, the cricket earns its keep.

The snowy tree cricket, *Oecanthus niveus*, serenades you from tree trunks and fence posts along suburban roads. It's a one-note musical trill, uttered about twice a second; sometimes without pause for half an hour. On warmer nights the cricket sings faster; on chilly nights it slows down. With a whole line of territory—a hedge, say, or an overgrown ditch along the road—the insects sing in unison. The effect, as you drive along, is that of one continuous cricket: churr-churr-churr, right beside your car, all the way.

Since the cricket's activity is governed by the temperature, it is possible to find how warm it is by listening to that song. The more chirps per minute, the higher the temperature must be. Count the number of chirps in fifteen seconds. Add forty—and the resulting sum is the temperature in degrees Fahrenheit. Thus, if you got thirty-two trills in a fifteen-second period, the total number when you add forty would be seventy-two—72 degrees. It works, too—give or take a degree. How the cricket will make the adjustment to the Celsius scale I do not know.

The snowy tree cricket is well named. Light creamy-green in color, it is conspicuous against the bark of the tree. It is hard to catch, however, for it bears the keen eyesight of all its family. Try to sneak up on it and it sidles around to the other side of the tree. Or, hard pressed, it flies into the upper foliage, where its light color enables it to disappear against the sky.

Crickets and grasshoppers don't sing with their mouths, as we do. They buzz, scraping wing against wing, or leg against wing. A male tree cricket sings with wings raised, using them as both fiddles and amplifiers. The song is probably for the benefit of other males, telling them to keep their distance. The female, it seems, is unable to hear the sound, as she apparently has no ears.

The male sends out an invitation to his potential mate from scent glands beneath his wings. As he raises those wings the glands are uncovered, spreading their perfume. She seems to have little difficulty separating his come-hither cologne from the other smells of the evening air. She jumps and flies to his side over bottles, through bushes, and one leap ahead of marauding cats. Arriving safely, she nibbles at those scent glands in what amounts to an engagement ceremony.

Crickets and their relatives scarcely begin to represent the insects to be found right around home, as it were, no matter where your home might be. A college friend of mine, taking a course in entomology, wondered how many species of insects lived in and about her apartment house and the tiny lawn that surrounded it in downtown Pittsburgh. I don't remember the total number, but Nancy collected more than fifty species from the windows alone. Moths, beetles and flies buzzed around them at night, trying to get in—and then, in the daytime, they struggled to get out again.

Earwigs, those persistent little European imports, trotted through the chinks in the foundation of the building. The ferocious-looking forceps at the rear of these insects makes them look dangerous, but it's all a sham. There is little basis to the old myth that they'll invade your ears if given a chance, either. About the only problem they caused around my friend's apartment building was their attacks on some of the bulbs and roots of the plants at the edge of the lawn. Plus the trauma on the part of the building supervisor when he discovered what she had found.

Nancy learned that the rug-sized lawn had attracted its own Lilliputian population. "The lawn is so small that a power mower doesn't even get warmed up before it's finished," she told me, "but to the insects it must smell as good as a golf course. I found chinch bugs on the grass, aphids and caterpillars in the hedge, flies all over the place, and half a dozen kinds of beetle."

One of the latter was a dead Japanese beetle, left over from the year before. She recognized it by its grain-of-corn size, bronze-green color, and white spots along the sides. "So I dug up the saddest-looking chunk of lawn I could find when the super wasn't looking. Sure enough, there were this year's grubs."

The C-shaped larvae of the beetle, feasting there in the dark, sometimes cut off enough roots so that the sod can be lifted like a mat. Sharing the meal with the grubs were several smooth, orange wireworms. Their parents, known as click beetles from their ability to snap into the air when placed on their back, are plant-eaters, too. Doubtless their attentions were not welcomed by the two little trees near the sidewalk.

Nancy also discovered the eggs of lacewing, or golden-eyed fly (*Chrysopa*), near a thriving assemblage of aphids. These are among the easiest of insect eggs to identify; each one is laid at the tip of a slender, hairlike stalk. The larva that hatches, it seems, is so voracious that it would consume its brothers and sisters if they weren't up in the air, out of harm's way. As it is, it often consumes its own eggshell. Then, running to the nearest supply of aphids, it chews them to bits.

You probably have seen the adult lacewing, by the way. It often flutters around street lights and windows at night. Gauzy-green and slender, it is about an inch long, with eyes the color of polished gold. It looks too fragile to withstand the scrutiny of the next bird—much less to have once been an aphis-lion, as the ferocious larva is called. But try to capture a lacewing and you discover its not-so-secret weapon. An overpowering stench arises from your cupped hand, and you drop the fly in dismay. The smell lingers, too, so that you—or a bird or a bat—remember not to let it happen again.

Inside the building Nancy found other apartment dwellers along with her human neighbors. Ladybird beetles, or ladybugs, like the cat that always wants to be on the other side of the door, constantly crawled along the windows, seeking a way out. Several species of these orange-and-black creatures spend the winter as guests in offices and dwellings. They often pay for their keep by consuming scale insects, mealy bugs, white flies, and other offenders among the house plants.

She also found carpet beetles, abroad on less commendable errands than the ladybugs. Their eggs, hidden in rugs and upholstery, hatch into hairy little grubs that dine on almost any material of animal origin. Feathers, fur, hides, woolens—even a fish carefully skinned and mounted on a plaque—may provide a carpet beetle condominium.

I remember one carpet beetle that livened up a summer when we were children. Or, to be exact, it helped calm it down. Irma, Jim and I lived with our folks in an old house in Connecticut. During the years, as the house had mellowed, it had gained a cadre of its own peculiar nonhuman residents. One of these was a talking pillow.

My grandmother had made the pillow, sewing an armful of feathers into a sack of stout muslin. Her stitches, although lovingly made, were not as close and regular as those done on a machine. Apparently an extra-wide stitch had allowed a carpet beetle to make its way inside. Or, if the beetle hadn't been able to gain entry itself, it had laid a few eggs in frustration near the opening. At least one larva found the feathery feast and spent the summer wallowing in plenty.

You could hear it wallow, too, if you lay perfectly still and listened while it moved about, a few inches from your ear. So, that summer, one of us would go to bed willingly—almost eagerly—when it came to our turn with "the Friendly Pillow," as we called it.

Carpet beetles, quite naturally, supply a share of the artwork that's attributed to moths. The little clothes moth (*Tineola bisselliella*) turned up in Nancy's collection from an unlikely spot: an upright piano. It seems that the felt hammers and the leather tabs of the "action" of a piano are fine places for the adolescence of this straw-colored little insect. The piano had been unused for years, and when a music-loving friend of the owner sat down to play, three or four notes refused to oblige. Opening the piano, he discovered several of the half-inch moths flying about in agitation. Their keyboard smorgasbord erupting all around them, they took to their wings until things settled down.

Actually, there's little use in going after a flying clothes moth. The larva is the destructive stage. One of the adult's first accomplishments after transforming from the cocoon is to mate and lay its eggs. Its business over, it then indulges in the delights of an airborne excursion. So by the time you see a clothes moth, it's probably too late.

Well, almost too late. There is a certain satisfaction in a hundred-fifty-pound human chasing down a ten-milligram moth. Satisfaction to the spectators too.

Most of the moths in that collection were gathered in the spring and early summer from obviously limited surroundings. Had there been just a bit more greenery or had the season been further advanced, she might have come up with several others. The hawk moths, for instance, are cosmopolitan in their habits. They may visit a suburban flower garden or even a window box. Built like a jet plane with narrow, swept-back wings, they are among our largest moths.

One, the hummingbird clearwing, hovers among flowers like its namesake. Its wings blurred in flight, it resembles a huge buzzing wasp. However, it is harmless as it visits petunias, nasturtiums and similar deep-throated flowers. Pausing in front of each, it uncoils its tongue for a sip. Then it backs away in mid-flight—an accomplishment mastered by few other insects.

Nancy might have collected one or two of the great Saturn moths, as well. These insects, some that will overspread the palm of your hand, often flutter to their death against the bright lights of the city. I recall attending a night ball game when the antics of several giant cecropia moths almost stole the show from the players. The moths would crash against the glaring lights and lose their equilibrium. Apparently knocked silly, they would fall toward the seats below. There, just as panicky fans ducked in apprehension, the dazed creatures would get their bearings, flap upward and repeat the performance.

Moths—and wasps and flies and beetles in the literal thousands—are in attendance around aircraft beacons, lighthouses and windows of people who work late at the office. They are there because they cannot help it. An insect flies toward a lamp because the muscles on the strongly illuminated side are weakened in some way. It tends to turn toward this weaker side. As a result, it flies in a diminishing circle right into the light.

Among the most faithful inhabitants of Nancy's collection vials were the ants. She found black carpenter ants, yellow sidewalk ants, red grease-loving ants, black sugar ants. The carpenter ants were mostly in the basement; their wanderings led in and out of a hole in the foundation. Probably an old timber or a stump was buried in the rubble outside the building. Carpenter ants excavate tunnels for their homes in wood of some kind; hence their name. They do not use wood as food in the manner of termites. Thus, although their appearance around the house may be unsettling, they are of less concern than the more secretive termites.

The sidewalk ants were found at ground level, too. Their little anthills, containing scarcely a tablespoon of soil, were flattened several times a day by pedestrians. Undaunted, the patient insects built them back again and again.

The little grease-loving ants were much more liberal in their favors. They consorted with the tenants on the top floor just as with the building supervisor in his basement kitchen. So did the tiny sugar ants, whose scientific name, for all its length, manages to convey an idea of the dimensions of its owner: *Monomorium minimum*. And, indeed, this is about the minimum among ants, for one of these little workers could fit comfortably within any of the three *o*'s in its name here on this page.

Ants are constantly being confused with termites. Perhaps a word about the latter is in order. Termites may, indeed, share your sills and joists and rafters—all quiet and unknown. It's hard to detect them, too, even if you know what to look for. Luckily, however, you can lessen your chances of falling through the parlor floor with a few simple precautions.

You can start by living in the northern United States or Canada. Termites are essentially warm-weather friends, and regard chilly climates with a significant lack of enthusiasm. Sometime, on one of our blustery Vermont nights when the wind shrieks, the temperature is way below zero, and the roads are impassable, perhaps I'll remember to say, through clenched teeth, "Good! No termites!"

Second, you can hazard a rough guess as to the potential extent of the termite population. Take an ice pick and jab it into a few beams and studs, especially around the cellar. If the timber is sound, you'll know it. If it looks sound, but the pick travels half an inch or more, better check further.

Third—and most important, from the standpoint of doing something positive—look for bridges between the ground and the building. Such bridges don't have to be extensive; just a discarded board leaning against a house will do. Or even a tree limb that broke off and fell, unnoticed, where it touches both house and ground. And a forgotten mound of earth, piled against the wood, is practically a red carpet. Termites must have contact with the soil, for without it their source of moisture is gone. Sometimes they even make a little tube of clay and sawdust running up the cement foundation. Look for such an engineering feat, too.

If you see even one termite, you can be sure there are more. In fact, in a way, there *is* no such thing as one termite—not for long, anyway. These little white insects, about the size of ants, live in colonies. Blind, soft-bodied, and helpless as individuals, termites place their strength in numbers. They have a queen, just like the ants, plus thousands of workers to excavate new galleries, feeding as they go. It's a neat arrangement, like a power shovel that uses its own earth for fuel.

One question that long puzzled scientists was how the termites could eat away most of the inside of a floor joist, say, while leaving the outside intact. The answer is apparently a matter of mechanics. As those sharp-jawed little workers chew through the wood near the outer edge of the joist, the fibers part with an increasing strain. As they approach the extreme outside—and a potential breaking point for the whole structure—the snap of each successive fiber gives advance warning. So the insects turn their attention to other edibles, leaving the joist still apparently whole and good—until you come along and move the refrigerator.

Once a year the termite colony goes out to seek greener—

or woodier—pastures. Since the whole tender-skinned family must stay in place or risk the danger of drying out, the exploration is put in charge of a group of specialists. These are winged males and females, armored in a cuticle that resists drying for a period, and possessing eyes so they can find their way through the unfamiliar upstairs world.

These winged adults, or reproductives, emerge by the thousands on a certain day of the year. Their point of exit may be the top of an old stump, if they have made a home in the decaying roots, or even a growing bush if they have lived in some hidden wood nearby. With your house or apartment they may choose a convenient clapboard or a handy doorsill.

Taking flight in such numbers as to look like a thin wisp of smoke, the reproductives circle upward. Other termites are becoming airborne the same day. The various flights mingle and mate in mid-air, thus helping to prevent inbreeding. Each new couple drops to earth, breaks off the now-useless wings and seeks a potential home site. Like a crop of seeds, many of them fall on unproductive ground. Others are snapped up by birds, frogs, lizards, spiders and snakes. A few, however—a very few I might add, or the world would be one great termitarium—find just the right conditions, and a new colony is on the way.

The ants also have an annual reproductive flight. You can tell the difference between ant and termite by observing the wings and the waist. Both pairs of termite wings are about the same length. The front pair of wings on the ant is longer than the rear pair, just as in its cousins the wasps, bees and hornets. Then, too, the ant has a more curvaceous silhouette. It is wasp-waisted, while the termite is definitely dumpy. The termite's waist is about as thick as the rest of its body.

Actually you do not need to be concerned about flying ants or termites, anyway. Not unless they emerge in the bathroom,

I suppose—as happened with a thunderstruck lady who telephoned me from Nashville. They are built for travel, so they are somebody else's worry. Of course, the home folks they leave behind are still *your* worry.

It is interesting, by the way, to consider our attitude toward all the creatures that have crawled, leaped and flown through this chapter. If we move in on them, that's all right; they must get out of the way. But let the tables get turned, let an adventuresome insect come up for a closer look, or let some creature gently remind us "I was here first," and we're in a panic.

Granted that there's a place for termites, you may still wonder what to do if *their* place happens to be *your* place too. In plain language, how do you get rid of them?

Unfortunately, my answer would have to be the same as the one I gave that lady from Nashville: "It's bigger than both of us." Get in touch with a competent authority. And if you're not sure who is competent, check with one of bureaucracy's best products, your local Agricultural Extension Service. Almost every county seat in America has one or more Extension Service agents, who have a wealth of information right at their fingertips. They may not recommend any one private source, but they can give you a list. Knowing the local situation, they can tell you what else to do, as well.

The Extension agent used to be almost an extra hand for the farmer while his feminine counterpart, the Home Demonstration agent, was much the same for the farmer's wife. They still are, too, in rural areas. They're available to you too, no matter if your "farm" is tilled by snowblowers, harvested by lawnmowers and fertilized by pigeons. You'll find the Extension agent under "United States Government" in your phone book. Or write your state university; the service is actually a cooperation of federal and state facilities. One agent, when asked for a simple definition of the service, said that "it's where the University comes to the people."

Pamphlets published by the Extension Service may also help guide your steps when it comes to those stinging cousins of the ants: the wasps and bees. Many of these creatures live in hives or nests and are termed social insects. Sometimes their sociality extends to include you—whether you wish to return the compliment or not. Their exquisite sense of smell tells them that there's a Sunday picnic at the park, or refreshment somewhere else. Gifted with an ability to find their way over miles of landscape, they sometimes forage at downtown fruit stands and carry their winnings out beyond the last bus stop.

Just one honeybee and a couple of hornets had made their way to my friend's building in Pittsburgh. On occasion, however, a whole hornet family may take up city life. One day I went to visit Mrs. Laura Perkins, a friend who lives in Bristol, Connecticut. Her apartment is one of four in a house just a few feet from a busy highway, Route U.S. 6. She lives on an active section of that highway, opposite a steak house and half a block from the entrance to a large shopping mall. All around her are stores, parking lots, businesses.

When I entered the hall and materialized at her living room door she looked at me in surprise. "How'd you get in?" she asked.

I indicated the entrance behind me. "Just walked right through the front door."

"Through all those hornets?"

Now it was my turn to be surprised. I hadn't noticed, but she pointed them out to me: a white-faced hornet's nest larger than a football. It was planked right against the window glass, just a few feet from the door.

"We've been using the back way," she said, "so nobody gets stung."

The hornet danger was low, I assured her, as long as they were not molested. But I didn't blame her for giving them a wide berth. It was an active nest, with hornets arriving and leaving constantly, sometimes in twos and threes. Pacifists they were, but the whitefaces still bore a terrible weapon.

We watched from inside the window as the hornets kept at their work. The central "honeycombs" of paper held dozens of small grublike larvae. The larvae hung head downward while the workers brought their food. Most of the food consisted of insects, chewed into hamburger and held by the adults so the youngsters could finish them. Several cells contained developing pupae; as soon as they transformed into adults, they would start right in on the household chores.

The outer half of the nest was built in more than a dozen layers. These layers were of a coarse paper, fashioned by the hornets from bits of wood chewed up with saliva. The layers were one hornet-width apart, so the insects could go between them. As the colony grew, an inner section would be torn away and used to help make the outermost shell. We could see half a dozen hornets stripping away the wallpaper, as it were, while an equal number added to the siding.

Parts of several layers were tinged with red. "That's Fred's old rowboat," Laura explained. "It's been rotting away in the back yard for years. We've watched hornets bite off chunks of it and carry them to the nest."

A streak of green, we learned, was part of a broken picnic table that had been bulldozed aside when the shopping center was built. There were also flecks of other colors—evidence that the hornets apparently exercised individual taste in finding just the right fibers, if not colors, for the job. The gray shade of the whole nest, we figured, was just the general hue of well-chewed wood.

I took a number of photographs of the nest on that August day. In early September I photographed it again; it had increased about a quarter in size. Later that month some pranksters knocked it down, leaving things in a fine state for the apartment dwellers the next day. However, the midnight marauders may have gotten more results than they had planned. Hornets can see silhouettes fairly well against the sky. Besides, with their keen sense of smell a few of them may have turned the tables on their tormentors.

The name *hornet*, by the way, refers to any social, paper-making wasp. There are solitary wasps too—the mud daubers and pottery wasps, for instance, who may make little clay domiciles in your rafters or under some projection of the building. Like the hornets, they catch insects—usually, caterpillars—to provision the nest for their young. Some species capture spiders, however, thus leading to official doubts as to their total effect on insect populations.

An occasional newspaper story will give an account of a nest of hornets in a car that's overparked, an attic, or a fireplace chimney. Honeybees may show up in similar places; however, their appearance is hailed with more rejoicing because of the honey they provide.

I recall one afternoon at Plymouth Central School when I was in the second grade. The whole school whooped out into the yard, after Eunice Sutliffe and another girl were stung by a couple of bees. The bees were members of a hive that had made its abode in a hollow tree next to the school entrance.

Mrs. Barry, our teacher, had a friend who was a beekeeper, so she called him to the rescue. While we watched in silent fascination, he and a companion smoked the bees into submission. They cut and pried away a loose slab of wood, lifted out brown combs of honey, and saved the whole school. I forget what they did with the bees, but the next day we were all treated to a big pan of gooey honey.

One of the "bees" collected by my friend in that apartment building turned out to be a clever case of mimicry. Several flies resemble bees so closely that even sharp-eyed birds leave them alone. Known as syrphid flies, they are striped yellow and black, just like honeybees. They even visit flowers and feed on the nectar. But, of course, they are only flies, with little capacity to harm you.

You can tell the difference between these two great groups of insects by counting the wings. Bees have four wings; flies but two. This important but little-known distinction was solemnly pointed out by our entomology professor. "And so," Dr. DeCoursey concluded, "if you want to tell if it's a bee or a fly, just pick it up in your fingers and begin counting wings. If you get as far as 'one' you've got a fly."

That striped little impostor had plenty of company of its own kind. Nancy discovered a couple of tiny fruit flies inspecting a wine bottle at the curb. Houseflies, gnats, green-bottle or carrion flies and several cluster flies buzzed at the windows.

Had it been winter instead of summer, she might have collected cluster flies by the quart instead of the dozen or so that she found. These flies, seeking winter shelter, make their way into buildings. They find such unorthodox entrances as knotholes, spaces between clapboards and even keyholes. Finding a friendly corner they gather by the hundreds in close-packed clusters; hence their name.

Cluster flies are harmless, even if they do upset your serenity by their zany aerial blunderings through the room on a sunny winter day. Come spring, they gather by the thousands again, but this time, happily, on the outside of the building.

Another fly that is not completely aware of where the country stops and the city begins is that long-snouted critter known as the mosquito. Nancy found three specimens. This, we figured, was a low count, considering the clever way in which mosquitoes have taken on city ways. They have adapted their aquatic childhood to such impromptu habitats as old cans and bottles filled with rain water; flower urns and vases in cemeteries; auto tires and hubcaps that ran away, often ending up with tiny puddles of their own. With a life span from egg to adult of only a couple of weeks, a skeeter can benefit from almost any shower, passing its apprenticeship in a pint-sized "pond" and emerging to enliven your existence when and where you least expect it.

There was one such mosquito right in an office building in downtown Manhattan. It accompanied me on the elevator all the way up to the twentieth floor. A taped orchestra played soothing music for the two of us. Then, as the elevator stopped I made my exit. The mosquito stayed just as it was, however. The last I saw as the door closed was that mosquito, resting quietly on the elevator wall, serenely enduring that serenade while it continued its yo-yo existence right beside what, I suppose, might have been its name: Otis.

Many of the other denizens of Nancy's insect collection would be of interest only to Nancy and her entomology professor. She even collected several kinds of spiders. These creatures, while not insects, are often associated with them. However, we'll dispense with the technical details.* The spiders, like the insects, were surprising in their numbers and variety. Little bulldoglike jumping spiders moved in tiny leaps on the outside of the building. A couple of yellow crab spiders clung to the center of the flowers in the border garden, camouflaged and waiting for an unwary fly. Small wolf spiders stalked their prey through the grass and along the sidewalk. Funnel-web spiders spread their silken handkerchiefs on the lawn, waiting for chance to toss them a meal.

These were just the outdoor spiders. More of their relatives lived inside, spinning webs in corners, beneath stairs, under washbowls and inside the cozy globes around electric lights. Luckily for the peace of mind of the other tenants who helped her make the study, there were no black widows, brown

* Let's just note that spiders have eight legs; adult insects six.

recluses or tarantulas. These three spiders, while admittedly the purveyors of poison, have long suffered from the effects of a smear campaign. Discovery of them in a building often results in anything from a broken lease to—as one jittery friend of mine termed it—having the house exterminated.

Tarantulas can be dismissed quickly. If they're in a building, it's usually by accident. In Southwestern towns they may come in out of the desert, while in less favored areas they have to ride in on a bunch of bananas from a cargo ship. Obviously neither circumstance is the usual thing—although Patty Hier, my secretary, once brought me a tarantula that had somehow survived fumigation and inspection of a fruit shipment from Ecuador. It had arrived, game but groggy, at a grocery warehouse in Burlington, Vermont.

That tarantula stayed with me two years, by the way. Its hairy body, with its saucer-width leg spread belied its placid nature. It never attempted to bite. Nor would the bite have been as bad as people seem to think, anyway. It's about like a bee sting—fiery, but hardly fatal.

The black widow has suffered from a sort of embarrassment of riches. She originally preferred dark, quiet places like the inside of hollow logs or the space under tipped-up stones. When we came along with all our cellars and sewer holes and outhouses, the black widow found new underworlds to conquer. Now she has been reported from nearly all of the contiguous United States and nearby southern Canada.

Latrodectus mactans is poisonous, true. And very much so. But she is timid and shy, and can hardly be forced to bite. She would much rather curl up in her nondescript web in that dark corner and wait until you went away. If she *did* bite, the effect on you could be anything from a mere pinprick through severe abdominal pains (several "appendicitis attacks" have turned out to be half-noticed black-widow bites) to death. But that last result is rare, indeed; there have been perhaps a hundred proven deaths in North America. You take greater chances than that every time you ride in a car. Still, better steer shy of any jet-black spider with a half inch body and a red or yellow hourglass marking on the underside. No point in being number 101.

The brown recluse spider has likewise suffered adverse publicity. Called the fiddleback spider because of the violin-shaped design on its body, *Loxosceles reclusa* is about the size of the black widow. It is found mostly in the South and the West. Like the black widow, it is—well, a hermit, a recluse. It seems inclined to associate with humans, but would rather get out of sight than stay and bite. Nevertheless, it *can* bite, with the same wide range of results as from a bite of the black widow. It has been nipping people for years, but few people heard about it in those good old days before radio and TV. Nowadays, let one brown recluse defend itself, and the whole world hears about the crime on the next newscast.

All told, you might as well not press your luck. If there's a chance of encountering even a harmless house spider, better check before you go reaching into dark corners and under furniture. After all, probably neither of you likes surprises. Not that kind, anyway.

One final apprehensive look at the spiders and their kin. Scientists call members of the spider family *arachnids*, after the mythical Arachne, the mortal seamstress who dared compete with the goddess Athena in weaving skill. Athena flew into a rage and changed her into a spider. Those fragile-looking characters known as daddy longlegs are also arachnids; you often find them wandering over grass and bushes. They're the scourge of mites, aphids and other lesser creatures.

An occasional scorpion—also an arachnid, even if it looks more like an undersized lobster—finds shelter around dwellings of the South and the West. With the exception of the

Durango scorpion (*Centruroides*) of Mexico and adjacent United States, whose two-inch length belies its sometimes-lethal wallop, the rare scorpion visitor should hardly be cause for dread. Respect, yes, but terror, no.

Over a wider range of North American homes, the little false scorpion makes its way up and down walls and across ceilings. It looks like an abbreviated scorpion—tailless and only a third the size of your little fingernail. Its minuscule pinchers, normally used to capture small insects and mites, waggle at you in defiance if you dare to come too close. I've seen this tiny pugilist in buildings from Toronto to the Gulf Coast. During World War II I found it on European walls too.

The ability to get around has always been a strong point with most arthropods ("jointed-legged," to translate this scientific term for insects, spiders and similar Tinker Toy creatures). Thus those thousand-legged worms, or millipedes, may crawl into almost any crack in search of their vegetarian meal—even if that crack turns out to be in a wooden pallet supporting a transoceanic shipment of goods. Centipedes, looking for more lively provisions, may sidle up next to those same millipedes, or may pursue their prey along miles of buried sewer pipe.

That same motility, doubled in spades, counts for all the eggs and young that these myriad creatures are forever leaving behind. At the end of a recent trip to study the bird life of Bermuda, I dropped in to say goodbye to my host, Dr. Wolfgang Sterrer of the Bermuda Biological Station for Research. "You're leaving that walking stick behind, of course," Wolfgang said with a grin, "or they'll confiscate it at customs."

I considered the three-foot length of Bermuda cedar I had picked up along the beach at St. George's. Just a piece of driftwood, I had figured; but Wolfgang shook his head. "Scale insects," he said. "They've killed most of the cedars here on the islands. Who knows what they'd do in Vermont?"

We scrutinized the piece of wood. In this case it was "clean." Several attached barnacles indicated that it had soaked in salt water for months. Not even the eggs or young of the scale, clamped under the turtlelike shell of their mother on the cedar bark, could withstand such a bath. But it caught me up short: well-meaning souvenir hunters, even those that may be petrified at the sight of a butterfly, must constantly supply first-class accommodations for all those little opportunists who merely await their chance. Science says there are approximately a million known species of insects alone, with perhaps another million or more yet to be identified. So, we must be providing some unwitting service every time we turn an ignition key, take out the garbage, or even toss away a cigarette butt.

Yes, a cigarette butt. Peg and I were visiting relatives in Birmingham, Alabama. Planning an impromptu picnic, we sat at an outdoor table near a hamburger stand. Waiting for some friends to arrive, Peg read a newspaper while I gazed at the contents of an automobile ash tray that someone had dumped on the ground. They must have tossed them in a hurry, too; the cigarette butts were scattered in a row about five feet long.

Mentally planning to scoop up the mess in a minute, I took the other half of Peg's newspaper and soon was absorbed in its contents. Then, remembering the cigarette trash, I went to pick it up. Now the line of stubs stretched about eight feet, and it was still growing.

Some enterprising ant, it seems, had found the mess. Whisking her antennae over the offerings, she made an interesting discovery: the filter tips tasted good. So, trotting back to the nest, she returned with reinforcements. Now, before my eyes, half the contents of that ash tray went bumping along over the patio and into the grass.

To a Vermonter this really should have been no surprise, even down in Alabama. One of the most faithful customers for Vermont's celebrated maple syrup is the tobacco industry. I remember trying Rum and Maple tobacco back in my college pipe-smoking days, as well as other flavorful blends whose names escape me. And today maple is used in some cigarette tobacco—including, apparently, the brand whose smoke passed through those discarded butts. Concentrating the sweetness in the filters, the butts were a lucky find for those fortunate ants.

I didn't find out the ultimate fate of those traveling tips, as the whole routine disappeared beneath a brick wall. Nor, I am sorry to say, did I learn exactly what brand of cigarette it was. With more presence of mind I could have notified the manufacturers of those cigarettes. I bet they would have been interested. Or, better still, perhaps I could have told the story to their competitors. *They* might have been interested, too.

Sometimes, to paraphrase Milton, you may serve if you just stand and wait. When I was in the Air Force we spent half our time, as I recall, standing at attention. One time at Maxwell Field in Alabama we lined up, row on row, for a general review. On the sleeve of each cadet was the Air Force patch: a colorful yellow-and-blue winged star with a bright-red center. While we stood stonily, eyes front, several butterflies drifted from one patch to another. Apparently unable to comprehend that none of these cloth "flowers" held a drop of nectar, the butterflies hopefully sampled the whole squadron.

While talking about insects, spiders and the like, I should give at least a brief nod to those other invertebrate critters, the snails, slugs and earthworms. Those snails and slugs (slugs, for our purposes, can be treated merely as shell-less snails) can also get around, for all their lethargic view of life. And earthworms may readily inhabit your garden and lawn, even if the "garden" is a windowsill flowerpot and the "lawn" a few sprigs of grass that sprang up when the canary seed got dropped on it.

Apparent helplessness and a willingness to run their lives in low gear have not hampered these soft-bodied creatures. The molluscan ancestors of the snails and slugs crawled through the primeval seas some half billion years ago. Ancestors of the earthworms got their start around that time, too. They have been inching through life ever since. So, as the tortoise proved, the race is not always to the swift.

You can see the glistening pathways of these creatures across a sidewalk after almost any dewy morning. Sometimes the day breaks faster and hotter than expected; then you may find them, curled and shriveled, at the end of the trail. But they may just be biding their time; sprinkle them with a garden hose, or let a sudden shower give them a welcome drink, and they'll revive. Soon they exude the slime that is both their protection against enemies and the slippery highway over which they can travel. Then they are off at a gallop for the life-giving shade of a pile of old leaves two feet away.

Earthworms provide a welcome service in almost any soil that will grow a plant. They tunnel through the soil, constantly consuming organic material and breaking it down into their version of fertilizer, which we refer to as "castings," when we see them on the surface of the ground. The whole upper layer of topsoil may be riddled and aerated with these passageways. In moist, tasty surroundings there may be as many as a million earthworms of all sizes per acre, or about thirty per cubic foot. An acre, by the way, is roughly the size of the playing surface of a football field.

In parched, sandy soil the numbers of earthworms may approach zero—active earthworms, that is. When conditions become inhospitable, each earthworm curls up as tightly as possible, thus conserving moisture. I've seen a backhoe, digging away in the thirsty earth of a summer day, uncover clusters of earthworms the size of a golf ball. Sometimes the worms are as much as three feet down from the dusty surface.

Snails and slugs are often regarded less favorably than those soil-enriching earthworms. For all their innocent appearance, these mollusks can accomplish surprising tasks. Each of them has a rasping filelike tongue, the radula, with which it scrapes away at chosen plant life.

Sometimes the owner of a fruit stand, having accidentally imported a few of these creatures on the bottom of an orange crate, say, finds his fruit sporting mysterious holes and pockmarks. Unable to discover the cause between customers, he locks the store at night, wondering if perhaps the supplier sent him a bad batch of fruit. The nocturnal slugs come out when things quiet down, and the next day the holes have turned to craters.

Luckily for the general walfare of his business, snails and slugs often keep gnawing away at a single spot instead of making a random sampling of all the fruit. If they visited the entire bin they'd spend the whole night traveling. They often find their meals by a sense of taste and smell. Thus, an already-breached cantaloupe may come in for a blistering campaign from every snail in the place, while its neighbors remain pure and unsullied.

Some of these mollusks were brought in by *escargotophages* —people who eat snails. The giant African snail, as big as a baseball, has been imported to our shores not once but a number of times. It *does* make good eating, too: Peg and I managed to corner a couple in Hawaii.

However, in our conservation-conscious world, the giant African snail is one recycling device we can do without. In its native Africa, it is held in check by various natural factors, but in California parks and gardens it transforms good topsoil into good (although largely unappreciated) *escargots* at the expense of tons of spinach and cabbage and petunias and artichokes. Other exotic snails brought to this country have shown less ebullience so far, but they can wait. After all, what's time to a snail?

On they go, then, these critters of all dimensions and dispositions who may join you, unbidden, even though the rules of your lease plainly specify "no pets."

So, as you spring to your feet there in your living room and stare at a dark object in the corner, repeat after me: Long live the invertebrates.

Judging from past history, they will, anyway.

5 · *The One That Got Away*

When you consider the good old days, you might conjure up a picture of square-built cars and meat markets with sawdust on the floor. In your picture there may be band concerts attended by people in funny clothes, wearing straw hats and carrying parasols. A streetcar clatters along Main Street. If it's early in the day, maybe the milkman and his horse are distributing bottles among the houses.

Sooner or later, if you dwell on the picture long enough, another character enters the scene. The new arrival could have stepped out of Huckleberry Finn, perhaps—or maybe it was yourself, back in those halcyon days of youth. Barefoot, sometimes, and with old clothes surmounted by a mop of tousled hair, you're whistling down the lane, going fishing.

Yep, you tell yourself, those were the days. The old fishing hole was just a few minutes' walk from that bandstand on the village green. Now that watery little heaven on earth has been filled in, paved over, built on. The stream that widened there to form a home for your finny prizes now runs along a well-littered ditch by the side of the street. Every so often it ducks into a culvert and crosses beneath the pavement. Then it continues on until it leaves town forever.

The water in that stream has departed, yes. And the fishing hole and the swimming hole that often went with it are likewise gone completely. True, some of the water may be recycled as rain, but the straightened and speeded-up stream will nevermore support those sagacious sunfish, those battling bullheads that threatened to break your cane pole—and tripled in size the instant they got away.

We'll never see such tackle-busters there again. But don't forget that fish are animate creatures with a will to live. All they may need is just half a chance and they are back in business. And, perhaps surprisingly, we are forever giving them that chance. For we cherish the watery world, you and I. We cling to it in everything from the tiny, unfurnished bowl with its single gulping goldfish to boat-strewn Crystal Lake there in the middle of town.

Although the swift-water trout and salmon and muskellunge could never abide the warmth and muddiness of many of our modern streams and ponds, not all their distant cousins are so hampered. There are fish—and a number of species, too—that do surprisingly well almost anywhere they can wet their gills. In spite of how we've channelized and culvertized their preferred waters, they have somehow managed to stay behind. They have even seized upon some foible of fate to return to an otherwise fishless world. Now and then such a lucky creature has refused to be flushed downstream, as it were. In a manner of speaking, it is the one that got away.

Take John White's bullhead, for instance. A bullhead, in case you haven't ever met one, is a small catfish, usually less than a foot long. Like other catfish it sports a mustache of eight feelers, or barbels, at the front of its head and around the mouth. I suppose this kind of catfish is called a bullhead because its head is big and bulky, like the massive front of a bull. Those feelers, although soft and delicate and gifted with an exquisite sense of taste to help it find food in murky water, look like a bull's horns. A bullhead may "bellow," too, on occasion—a little grunt of protest made by gulping air when it's removed from the water.

John White and I were fishing buddies in our boyhood days. We knew every submerged log and hidden stone in Scopino's Pond—later renamed Lake Plymouth as the little Connecticut town grew up around it. John could skitter a pork rind over the lily pads so that it hardly got wet—until some lunker of a pickerel smashed at it from below. He also knew how to parlay a fistful of earthworms into a pailful of tender, sweet bullheads; and one of these little catfish led an astonishing life because of John's prowess with hook and line.

We had caught a good mess of bullheads one evening and tossed them into a tub in the back of my little farm truck. Two wet burlap bags went over the tub to keep the fish moist until we got home. Then, since the hour was late, we decided to clean them in the morning. John was supposed to wake me by phone in the morning, or I was supposed to awaken him—I'm not sure which way it was. At any rate, neither of us gave those bullheads any thought, but merely got up and went to school at our usual time. Halfway through the morning we remembered our forgotten task. What kind of mess would our mess of bullheads be when we got home? Even though the truck was parked in partial shade, those fish would be steamed and spoiled after such a warm May day.

After school we hurried home, hoping to salvage at least a couple of the forgotten fish. Feeling our guilt and expecting our loss, we pulled back the upper layer of burlap, now dry and stiff.

The second layer was still a bit moist. Just as we reached for it, the burlap gave a little jump. Hastily snatching it away we stared at our supposedly rotten fish. And they stared right back at us—or at least some of them did. Still alive although they had been out of water some eighteen hours, half a dozen of the twenty bullheads gasped at us accusingly.

It was the second burlap bag that had saved the day. Because there had been enough dampness to moisten their leathery skins and the gills within their close-fitting flaps, those six had survived.

We quickly soused the whole lot in water. Most of them lay belly up, beyond hope. The six, however, managed to right themselves. Gulping the welcome water, they slowly worked the stiffness out of their muscles. In a few minutes they were gracefully swimming around in the tub, awaiting our next move.

We decided that they had had enough. No fishes deserved their freedom more than these. So we transferred them to a pail that wouldn't slop over in the truck and drove back toward the pond. Down into Plymouth we drove, past the grange hall and past the store. As we turned the corner around the old watering trough and started up South Street, John suddenly asked me to stop.

He pointed to the watering trough, left over from the days when travelers stopped to refresh their horses before going on their way. "Why not put a couple of bullheads in there?" John asked.

It seemed like a great idea. The trough was made of rough-laid stone, with plenty of shelving spots to hide a fish. So we selected two of the liveliest bullheads and lowered them into the water. Then we drove the two miles up to the pond and released the rest.

And it *was* a great idea, too. One of the bullheads was apparently worse off than we had figured, because we found it dead a couple of days later. The other one, however, lived on in that watering trough for more than a year. It found a projecting rock just the right size to hide under, and it soon became the unofficial pet of half the town.

It became a ritual to toss a worm or two in for "Andy Gump," as the whiskery fish was known in honor of a comic-strip character. Becoming aware of your approach, Andy would drift up to the top of the water and gulp a welcome. Then you'd dangle the worm in the water and that cavernous mouth would snap it out of your fingers. Doubtless the occasional saddle horse that paused for refreshment got more than expected; Andy would snap at almost anything.

He outgrew his rock, too. About six inches long when we put him in the trough, he nearly doubled his size in that year. Now, when he tried to hide under that rock, either his head or his tail would stick out. Philosophically, he allowed a bit of each to project. It didn't really matter how clumsily he hid himself; he had no enemies, anyway.

Andy might have lived a long and eventful life in that watering trough had it not been for the march of progress. Unknown to many of the town's residents—or at least to us kids, who could have done something about it—the center of Plymouth was due for a change. Bradley's Store, right on the corner of the intersection, was to give way to a gasoline station. The intersection itself would be widened and modernized, with a traffic-light chandelier hanging over Andy's living room.

Or, rather, the place his living room used to be. For some unknown reason, that watering trough was the first to go. We found it lying by the side of the road one afternoon, cracked and empty. When the workmen appeared, we learned later, the trusting bullhead, expecting his usual handout, rose to the surface and was scooped out, flopping, onto the street.

And what happened to him? We inquired until we found the man who had picked him up. "Oh, that fish?" said the man in response to our question. "Boy, was it *good*!"

And so our bristle-faced pal went down to defeat at last. But even though the town has changed and the times have changed, anglers young and old will continue to feel a twinge of remorse when some doughty catch proves hardier than expected. Chastened at the thought of a deed so dark as disinheriting a fish, they will sneak it into somebody's garden pool. Or they will simply swing around past Crystal Lake on their way home from fishing, and release it among all those paddle boats and canoes.

Then, some day, a hopeful Isaac Walton, more wishing than fishing, is startled by a genuine bite. Hastily hauling in, he lands his unusual prize on the well-clipped and power-mowed "beach." There he enjoys his own small moment of glory, right there in Memorial Park.

Such, by the way, seems to be the case every little while in at least three pools I know of. Each of these is surrounded by hordes of people. In these pools you'd expect the splash of a discarded can or bottle, yes, but hardly that of a feeding bass or pickerel. Yet these three ponds—one in New York City's Central Park; another in Forest Park in Springfield, Massachusetts; and the Duck Pond in the zoo at Crossett, Arkansas—continue to yield a tiny but steady crop of fish.

When the dam at Mirror Lake sprang a leak, right in the middle of the campus at the University of Connecticut, even the zoology department was surprised. The profs had never dreamed that the acre of water held so many fish. The mud fairly boiled as its scaly inhabitants jostled each other in the few deep holes that were left after most of the lake had drained away.

There are other ways to populate such island ponds, so to speak, besides the practice of people who catch fish and then are sorry. The ones who are not sorry may have their part in it, as well. One of the most popular lures is that which wiggles and plunges and tries to get away, thus stimulating pursuit: the live bait fish. Often such bait is a simple shiner or minnow. Sometimes, however, it may be the young of some other fish, caught in the seine or minnow trap.

Carefully suspended from a hook, such a youngster may struggle hard enough to escape. Or a sudden yank on the line may tear the hook right out of its body, leaving it with a painful but superficial wound. The frightened fish heads for cover. There it slowly regains its health—and the pond has a new resident.

Then, too, there's always the urge to experiment. If a nice, *silvery* minnow will tempt those lunkers, what'll a nice, *golden* one do? So a few goldfish, purchased at the local pet store, go on the hook for variety. One friend of mine, gifted with imagination and spare cash, claims that she has tried various colorful tropical fish, too.

The tropicals, doubtless, seldom survive the first frost; the goldfish may enjoy a better fate. Indeed, more than one pond bears signs posted along its borders clearly prohibiting the use of goldfish as bait. Goldfish on their own in a pond may reach a weight of two pounds or more. In accomplishing such a feat, they tear up the weeds and muddy the water.

So one angler may unintentionally provide the fish for another. Even if not a single bait fish gets away by accident, it's a temptation at the end of a day's fishing to toss the whole remaining contents of the minnow bucket into the pond—goldfish, guppies and all.

Other anglers besides the human variety may have a hand in the relocation of fish. Ducks, geese, herons and shore birds of many kinds sozzle through the shallows after roots, water insects and other dainties. In so doing they may accidentally pick up a few fish eggs. It seems that the eggs of many fish are laid in long sticky strings or gooey masses that may cling to a leg or a beak. Carried along on some feathered host, especially on a rainy day so they are kept moist, the eggs are thus airlifted to any waterhole that the bird may choose.

There's another way that birds can carry fish around. It's

quite unplanned, and both the bird and the fish are under protest, but I saw it work at least once. The fish in question, despite other plans it may have had, found itself in the company of a little green heron. This brown-and-olive bird, looking like a long-necked, spear-beaked chicken, came over the tops of the trees and landed in front of us as we canoed along the Peace River in Florida. It was obviously in distress, with some kind of a knot or bulge on its bill.

As we watched, the bulge straightened out. Our binoculars showed that it was the latter two thirds of an eel. Instead of obligingly sliding down the heron's throat in the manner of lesser fish, that plucky and pliable eel had thrown a half hitch around the bird's beak, Then, pulling for its life, it tried to haul its slippery self out to freedom. With every swallow it lost ground, but the heron couldn't gulp fast enough.

Finally the eel managed to break free. With a defiant shimmy, it flipped itself away, landed in the water at the heron's feet and slithered to safety in its new home, while the heron stabbed ineffectually at the ruckus stirred up in the mud as the eel retreated.

Few fish, of course, are as limber as an eel. However, such failings may be compensated for by the bird itself. If you have ever come close to the nest of a gull or a tern, as I have, you may be startled by the ability of some birds to divest themselves of their last meal. You are apt to be impressed by their accuracy too. While such a meal, when regurgitated, may be in a state of collapse, it is possible that freshly caught morsels could thus hastily be disposed of—especially if they wiggled or chewed, or tied themselves in eel-knots, or proved an embarrassment in some other way.

The eels, incidentally, can even provide their own transportation. I'm not referring to the sucker-mouthed critter known as the lamprey, which sometimes hitches a ride on ships, barges or large fish. Such creatures need wide expanses of deep water, plus clear streams for the depositing of their eggs. The eel in question is the American freshwater eel. *Anguilla rostrata* is about as resourceful a fish as ever slithered, twisting and flailing, over the side of a boat at the end of a fishline. Finding a dam or waterfall in the way of its migration upstream, the eel merely waits for a rainy night. Then, snaking over the wet ground, it bypasses the obstacle and eases itself into the water again. Thus almost any pond may provide a home for an eel.

A number of fish besides the eel can live out of water for several minutes in the rain, but few of them can actually make any progress as they flop around on the bank. No such limitations hamper the walking catfish, however. This import from southeast Asia has made itself at home in warm-water ponds, ditches, and even flower-rimmed pools on Southern estates. It often becomes a nuisance, eating the eggs and young of other fish. Like the eel, the walking catfish can go from one water hole to another as the mood strikes it. It wriggles and flops along, sometimes pulling itself forward with its fins.

Even the fish that never intentionally leaves the water can respond to the lure of new horizons. To many fishes the flow of any current apparently presents a challenge. And well it might, for even a slow drift, if not counteracted, would do a fish out of its home. Scientists feel that the detection of such currents may be an important task of the lateral line that runs along each side of a fish from gills to tail. Thus any pond with a flowing outlet is forever holding out an invitation to its finny neighbors further down the line. Often they merely point their noses into the current. Other times they dash themselves to death trying to climb all the dams and rapids in the whole stream.

On the other hand, a sudden flood or break in a dam may transplant the whole aquatic assortment from one pond to another. Such an event happened a few years ago in the little river that runs past my home.

The river had its headwaters in a beaver dam. The dam had

been in existence as far back as anybody could remember. The pond's furry inhabitants kept the dam in good shape, repairing every break as soon as it happened. As successive beaver generations practiced their skills the pond got larger, until it covered some fifty acres behind a bulwark that stood ten feet high.

About twelve years ago the beavers suddenly left. Perhaps they were trapped out; perhaps they merely moved away. At any rate, the dam fell into disrepair. As the sticks and twigs out of which it was woven began to decay, little leaks appeared. The leaks grew larger until, following the pressure of a week's steady rainfall, the dam suddenly gave way.

Weeds, silt and fish tumbled downstream with whoosh. The New Haven River, already swollen with rain, became a muddy torrent. It leaped over its banks, cut across curves in its own channel and raged all night. In the morning the little road that accompanied it in its valley sagged perilously in several places, and one of Lincoln's bridges sported a rakish angle as it dared anyone to cross.

The fishing was different along the way, too. After the river had subsided to a clear, swift trout stream again, a friend of mine decided to try his luck. Dropping the bait in the lee of an enticing rock, he got a bite. Setting the hook, he prepared to battle his trout. But the "trout" wouldn't cooperate. Instead of splashing and leaping and dancing on its tail, it hung in that pool like an old sock. When my friend finally extricated it, his prize turned out to be a pond shiner ten inches long. Scarcely more than what is known as a "trash" fish in trout circles, it was a whopper for its own kind—and, perhaps, glad in a way that its ordeal in those wild rapids was over at last.

Other anglers could tell similar fish stories. For weeks that river yielded yellow perch, pumpkinseed sunfish and bullheads —all unwilling escapees from that defunct beaver pond.

Trout streams are more of the country than of the town,

of course, but one of the features of almost any body of water is that it is never completely self-contained. Rains come and dams leak and water birds seek greener—or muddier—pastures. Thus, there's a chance that you'll never be sure about what lurks in the depths of anything larger than a drinking fountain.

Some fish are eminently qualified to take up a pioneering life. The carp from the Old World is a good example. Hailed as a wonder fish back in the 1870's and brought here in hopes that it would provide a cheap and abundant source of protein, *Cyprinus carpio* did just what was expected of it. Guzzling through the weeds and mud of any puddle where it was stocked, it seemed to thrive on anything. Snails, aquatic worms, roots of water plants, algae—all were accepted by the carp. Within just a few years a fingerling might reach a weight of twenty pounds or more. Some ponds, rich in edibles, produced several hundred pounds of fish per acre. All that remained, the carp's fanciers were assured, were the simple details of harvesting and taking to market.

They were taken to market, all right, but there were few buyers. Somehow that great fish, complete with huge, glittering scales, turned-down mouth and mustache of two pairs of drooping barbels, failed to excite the appetite as it lay staring at customers from its bed of crushed ice. Even when partitioned into unrecognizable cuts that bore such names as silversides or rainbow fish, it failed to live up to expectations. Nor could the average angler work up much enthusiasm about the fish. After the first flurry of activity, it often came in at the end of the line like some kind of gigantic tea bag.

Meanwhile, the carp kept right on its way, groping after aquatic edibles, uprooting weeds and muddying the water. So, after it had been introduced into playground pools, golf-course water hazards, ponds big and little, and even drinking troughs for livestock, the fish found itself in disfavor. Indeed, in many ponds in the early 1900's it became a misdemeanor to have anything to do with the fish—except, of course, to do away with it once you had caught it.

In addition to a digestion that allows it to find nourishment almost anywhere but in a swimming pool, the carp has another redeeming feature—at least it's redeeming from its own point of view. In keeping with other fish that have successfully eluded almost everything we have tossed at them, the carp can rise to the surface to gulp air.

A feat like this is handy in case the water is polluted. It's a lifesaver in a pond loaded with chemicals, or just plain lacking in dissolved oxygen. The eel and catfish too can do this trick. So can those little ditch-dwellers known as killifish and topminnows. So, too, can the goldfish, which is really a civilized cousin of the carp anyway.

Such fish actually take in a bubble of air. They absorb its oxygen through membranes connected with the throat and burp the spent air out with the next gulp. The whole process is almost like a simple lung. This is often why a forlorn goldfish can survive in a dirty, undersized bowl whose surface scarcely allows normal exchange of air with the atmosphere. It's not so much that the unhappy creature can live under such circumstances; it just takes it a long time to die.

Water that is laden with foreign matter and pollution not only is apt to be low in oxygen content; it also may be warmer than clear water. The suspended particles catch the sunlight and become heated, thus raising the temperature of the liquid around them. Fish in such waters must be able to stand the heat.

Chilly-water fish like trout, salmon and smallmouth bass have little chance in such a situation. Those carp and eels and catfish can do better. So can perch, sunfish, crappie and largemouth bass—provided, of course, that there's enough food to support them.

Most of the other chapters present a list of the living things in a certain group that might be expected to survive there in the shadow of the skyscraper or the soldiers' and sailors' monument. In the case of fish, as you must have gathered by now, such a task is harder. Or, perhaps I should say, it is easier. As long as people tinker with their surroundings the way they do, and as long as most of us find ourselves fascinated with the watery world in one way or another, there's a chance that any puddle big enough to cover a fish's back might become the abode of almost any fish you could name.

As an example, take the case of the reversing gar fish. Peg and I discovered the fish when we lived in Tallahassee, Florida, where I was taking flight training during World War II. The gar lived a few blocks from us in a narrow ditch along a street. This fish, in case you are not familiar with it, is shaped like a cigar with its snout prolonged into a toothy beak. Probably someone had thoughtfully dropped it into the ditch when it was small; now it was fully three feet long.

A three-foot fish in a two-foot ditch would find it hard to turn around—unless the fish was an eel. But the gar was certainly no eel: its hard, diamond-shaped scales, imbedded in its skin like hundreds of bony plates, offered great protection, but allowed little more motion than if the fish had been wrapped in the Sunday paper.

We contemplated its probable fate in that ditch. Many small minnows surrounded it; doubtless some paid tribute each day with their lives. A short rush, a snap—and there would be one less minnow. But each rush must have brought the gar closer to the end of the ditch. When it ran out of space straight ahead what did it do? Swim backward to the point of beginning and start all over?

The question remained unanswered for a couple of weeks. Then, when I got a few minutes off from duty, we decided to take a walk over to the ditch again. To our surprise, the gar was headed in the opposite direction. Somehow, it had turned around. But where?

Searching the gar's block-long bailiwick, we found no pool

wide enough to allow it to negotiate a turn. But then Peg noticed an interesting change in the fish's attitude in the water. Something near the bottom apparently caught its interest and it nosed down for a better look. In a minute it was standing nearly on end.

There, of course, was our answer: the gar could turn around anywhere it chose merely by pirouetting on its head or tail. The ditch was four or five feet deep—enough, probably, to last our snag-toothed friend the rest of its life. If the minnows held out, that is.

With such unlikely fish making the most of whatever the fates may afford, a list of possible residents of almost any pool could read like a piscatorial Who's Who. Of course, the actual number is far less than the theoretical. But I guess that's part of the lure of angling, whether it's a couple of kids headed out to the old fishing hole or it's you with your fancy Orvis rod, ostensibly teaching some youngster the tricks of the trade in Downtown Lake.

You never can tell what might turn up. Not for sure, anyway. Life in a watery community, fraught as it is with change from one day to the next, is—well, fluid, so to speak.

6·*Play It Cool*

SOME PEOPLE THINK those voices come from a kind of bird. Others guess more correctly and say they come from frogs, but from baby ones. It hardly seems possible that such a thin, piping call could be made by a full-grown adult.

However, adult frogs they are, even if they are only about an inch long. In most ways those spring peepers are merely miniatures of the familiar pond frogs—clammy skin, goggle eyes and all. They differ in their Lilliputian size when fully grown, in the warm brown of their coloration, and in the remarkable sticky disks on their tiny toes.

Spring peepers live primarily in wooded areas. Those sticky toe pads allow them to cling to the underside of a leaf high above the ground, or even to launch fearlessly out into space from one tree to another. Their small size and high motility serve them well as they scramble among the branches above an elm-shaded boulevard, or pounce upon a tasty insect in a grove of bushes at the edge of an abandoned lot. Their brown color matches dead leaves and grass so well that we are seldom aware of them in summer. Only in the spring, when they congregate in almost every little ditch and puddle, do we listen in amazement—"Now where did all those peepers come from?"

You may hear these little amphibians over much of the entire eastern half of the United States and adjacent southern Canada. City or country, it matters little to the elfin creatures. One year I heard my first peeper of the season on a March day while I was walking in New York City's Central Park. Another spring found me in Punxsutawney, Pennsylvania, on Groundhog Day, listening to a single peeper while we shivered in the dawn's light and waited for Punxsutawney Phil.

The redoubtable national groundhog appeared right on schedule, blinked at his shadow, and retired for six weeks more of winter, while the optimistic peeper went right on calling from a little swamp down there below the foot of Gobbler's Knob.

Optimism seems to be the key word for the peeper. Although it sings most lustily in the spring mating season, I have heard its hopeful chirp as far north as Connecticut every month of the year. Our sterner Vermont winters usually silence it during January, however. Nevertheless, it may pipe at the waning sun almost until Christmas and welcome it back during a February thaw.

There are several members of the genus *Hyla*, scattered over much of North America. The spring peeper, marked as it is with a dark brown X over the lighter reddish brown of its general body color, has been named *Hyla crucifer*—the "wood spirit that bears a cross."

But it bears it cheerfully. In balmy weather it may sing all night. As with most of the amphibians, it's the male that makes the noise. In a way it is an old, old song, harking back to one of the first spring songs ever heard on this earth—the croak of some energetic amphibian, celebrating the vertebrates' new release from the bonds of water.

Having crawled upward from the haunts of their finny relatives, those first amphibians were probably little more than creeping fish—gulping air and dunking themselves repeatedly to keep their skins moist. But within those clumsy bodies were the seeds of the crawling salamanders, the leaping frogs and toads, the alert and active lizards and snakes, and even the great dinosaurs. They were yet eons away from the birds and mammals, which were freed of direct dependence on the sun's heat as they carried their "climate" along with them in the warmth of their bodies.

Now, as then, however, the amphibians and reptiles must rely forever on the friendly sun. Its warmth tempers their surroundings, so the chill is removed from their bodies and they can operate normally. Thus the yelp of the tiny spring peeper is not only an announcement of his availability to members of the opposite sex, but in a way it's also a salute to the sun: "Welcome back!"

The triumph of the peepers as they mate and lay their eggs in the chilly spring waters soon spreads to other amphibians. These creatures too may have eked out a living almost under your nose. They have lived in roadside ditches, cemetery fountains and playground ponds until their once-a-year exuberance spills forth in song. Then you may hear the guttural croak of the spotted leopard frog, the clicking call of the cricket frog, the musical rattle of the chorus frog and the plinking banjo of the green frog.

Later, as the water warms, you may hear the bellow of a bullfrog. Like the bass fiddle in an orchestra, it's a background against which the other tunes are played. In spite of their seeming independence, all the amphibians must visit the water once a year to lay their eggs. Thus the smallest pool annually takes on the dimensions of an amphibian Mecca.

The toads too join the frogs in their springtime junket. With their dry and warty skin, toads can endure the parched summer better than frogs. They fan out from their native pool to the edge of your garden, the flower bed along your sidewalk, or the shelter beneath the bleachers at the local ball park. They may stay there several years. Sometimes they're isolated forever by new high-rise buildings or a cloverleaf intersection that replaced the swamp where they were hatched out as tadpoles.

Toads, however, seem philosophical about it all. Caught in a basement, they may shift from a diet of earthworms and butterflies to one of spiders and millipedes. If a decrepit building is pulled down around their ears it matters little. They keep right on snapping up insects—sallying forth nightly from beneath the shelter of a forgotten work glove or the discarded lid of a paint bucket. And one toad that our family knew personally spent an entire summer, evening after evening, squatting in the grass outside our living room. With almost no effort at all the toad lived high on the hog, flipping insects into its mouth as fast as they crashed against the lighted window and fell to earth.

Adaptability—that's the key, over and over, to one creature's success and another one's failure. "It's like the difference between a stout old tree and a tender sapling," a naturalist once told me. "The tree is the stronger, but the sapling has more bounce. It bends to earth in a storm and then it comes back. The tree cracks and breaks. Other living things are like that, too. Some can 'give,' but some cannot. The ones that can adjust to civilization, that can learn to live with us and our machines and our by-products will get along in our modern world. In fact, they may well outlast us. The others will fall by the wayside."

This ability to adjust may extend to some of those other amphibians, the salamanders. According to an old myth, a salamander was a creature that could live in fire. An occasional log, tossed on the blaze, may have sheltered a salamander under its loose bark. Driven out by the heat, the distraught creature fell into the fire but, protected by the moisture of its body, may have wriggled to safety. Hence the belief that salamanders can endure all four of the natural elements of air, earth, water and fire.

Some of these little four-legged amphibians do, indeed, seem to have a remarkable hold on life. Such tenacity is due, in part, to that moist skin. The slippery coating not only allows a salamander to escape an enemy, but often secretes a distasteful slime. This slime, similar to that produced by many frogs and toads, may actually kill a would-be predator —or, at least, remind the frustrated predator to mend its ways.

The moist skin serves another use in salamander life. Laced with blood vessels, it acts as an auxiliary lung. Indeed, there are salamanders that have no lungs at all, but merely transfer oxygen and carbon dioxide back and forth through the moist skin membrane. So, while they are slow and stodgy, salamanders really can live out of their accustomed element for a while—even though the ashes of a fire are definitely not recommended.

Then, too, their secretive habits often keep them from harm. Not much can happen to a salamander in its nook beneath an old board or an auto tire. And since nearly every insect and spider that moves may be the next meal, the little amphibian hardly ever needs to leave its hideaway.

Salamanders come in a variety of life styles. Some are fully aquatic, like the wrinkled hellbender of our large Midwestern rivers. Nearly as big as a baseball bat, it's occasionally hauled ashore at a city dock where it's exhibited like a sea monster. Somewhat smaller is the equally aquatic mud puppy. The mud puppy, often a foot long or more, may come in at the end of a fisherman's line in almost any lake or stream from the Great Lakes to the mouth of the Mississippi. Gifted with external feathery gills and an ability to eat almost anything, the mud puppy can survive in all but the foulest canals, right into cities and towns.

There are several smaller water-living types, too; you may see them beneath logs and stones of almost any stream. Less aquatic is the pond salamander, or newt (*Diemictylus viridescens*). Although it begins life as a swimming larva, it soon transforms to an air-breathing stage. Then it wanders around for a couple of years as a little red eft. With every rain, the adolescent newt crawls out by the hundreds on lawns and highways almost anywhere from Quebec to Florida, east Texas to Minnesota. Then, after two or three summers, it slips into a pond once more. There it changes to the familiar olive-green adult with sulphur-yellow belly and tiny red spots.

Still less tied to the water are several species of spotted salamanders (*Ambystoma*). Known as tiger or marbled or spotted salamanders according to their color pattern, these creatures live in dark places on land. They visit the water only during the breeding season. They are fairly large amphibians, too—sometimes eight inches or more in length. Their spotted pattern, plus a disconcerting habit of appearing in window wells of cellars, and eventually in the cellars themselves, has jolted many a family. Each spring I can count on two or three calls for help from someone who is terrorized by one of these harmless creatures. Then I go collect the "lizard" in the basement and take it out into the country.

True lizards, of course, may look like salamanders, but there are several differences. Lizards have a dry, scaly skin. They also have five toes on each foot, complete with claws. They have ear openings too, even though many lizards seem oblivious to sound. A lizard may quickly part with its tail when captured. The severed appendage writhes and thrashes so as to attract its enemy while the abbreviated lizard escapes.

Salamanders have none of these refinements—well, almost none, for a roughly handled salamander can lose its tail. Like the lizard, it can grow a replacement, however, and if it has to, a salamander can also grow a new arm or leg.

A few true lizards may take up city residence. One little *Anolis*, or Carolina lizard (*Anolis carolinensis*), crept through the branches outside our window when Peg and I were guests of Fred and Peggy Spencer in Columbus, Georgia. Occasionally it even leaped over to the windowsill and basked in the sun. When it was in the greenery its color was a leafy green, but often when it got on the darker colors of the house the "American chameleon" turned almost brown in three or four minutes.

Sometimes it got its signals crossed, especially when it was frightened. Once we tried to capture it. As it dashed about desperately, it adopted what was apparently the "color" of its agitated state of mind: a shocked, bright green.

Other anoles, plus swifts, skinks and fence lizards, may run through the bushes and along old trees and walls of estates and city parks. In the Southwest they may be joined by those odd little insect-catchers known as wall lizards, or geckos. In some parts of the world geckos are almost as much a fixture of the home as the furniture. Their large eyes, the round discs on their toes, and their habit of scouting the walls and ceilings for insects make them a conversation piece all by themselves.

Since most little lizards seldom enter houses on any but commendable purposes, they are often tolerated—indeed, sometimes encouraged. One of the first apartments Peg and I rented during the war was outside an air base in Florida. The landlady showed us around the place, pointing out all the facilities, and ending with a significant reference to two small lizards by the screen door at the rear of the building. "There's your lizards," she informed us, as if she was showing us a refrigerator. "They'll keep the cockroaches down for you."

Speaking of Florida, an occasional giant relative of the

lizards makes its way into the haunts of humans. Barbara and Roger Johnson of Lake Alfred showed us a development in a nearby town where the back yards of all the homes bordered on a canal. This canal, in turn, connected with a fairly large lake. The day before we arrived, a seven-foot alligator had cruised up to the very end of the canal, surveyed the apprehensive humans along the bulwarks, and nonchalantly cruised away again.

"There's never been a report of an unprovoked attack by an alligator on a human being," Barbara reminded us.

Peg considered the probable result of an encounter with a seven-foot saurian in its own element. "So who'd be left to make the report?" she asked.

I remember another alligator, too. This one was years ago, in Orlando, Florida. A flying buddy and I had called the airport tower for landing instructions. "Landing is on Runway 3," was the reply. "Only hold your position for a few minutes. We have an obstruction on the runway."

We were close to the field, so we flew over to see for ourselves. There was a radio-controlled jeep in the middle of the runway. It was parked near what looked like a large log. "We'll have 'im off the runway in a hurry," the jeep driver cheerfully assured me on the radio.

I saw a man get out of the jeep. He was followed by another. They cautiously walked to the "log," which switched itself violently into a sudden letter *U*. Both men fled to the jeep. Then there was silence. More silence. And more.

Finally the driver came back on the air. His voice had lost its confidence. "Well, he's pretty big—" he began, and trailed off.

So I got an alternate clearance from the tower and landed on another runway. I never did find out how the men got out of that little dilemma, but I bet the final decision was made by the alligator.

Alligators and lizards seldom stay long where it's very civilized. The same may be said for their relatives, the snakes. Only a handful of these reptiles can manage to find a living in the city. Most have been banished forever, perhaps in memory of the tale of that heinous deed in the Garden of Eden when sin first entered our lives. Since that time, nearly every hand has been against the serpent. After all, a critter that perpetrates such an act deserves little sympathy. "Sin, we hang on to," said the old preacher, "but the serpent has got to go."

The few snakes still found within city limits can get by because of their debonair food habits, perhaps, or their discreet way of life. After all, you cannot have much of a quarrel with a creature that you hardly ever see. Nor can you find much fault with its diet of earthworms, insects, or almost anything else that crawls. If an occasional mouse is taken, so much the better. And since the poisonous species have long since had their comeuppance in settled areas, there is little to worry about, anyway.

Nevertheless, an occasional snake, willing to forget history, throws its fortunes in with ours. Such was the case with one snake I met as I took a leisurely stroll. Everyone mindful of the landscape, or cityscape, has done the same as I did that morning, I'm sure: pick up a scrap of junk in the street and take it off to the nearest trash barrel. That's what I did, too —or what I meant to do. Seeing a discarded beverage can in the grass I gathered it up and took it with me.

Strolling along absent-mindedly, I almost forgot what I had in my hand. Then, as I swung my arms with each stride, I began to realize I was not alone. Something was in the can. The container felt heavy, but I had assumed that it was half full of soil or caked mud. However, mud didn't ordinarily rustle and thump and shift position like that. Certainly not when you held the can steady in your hand.

Pineapple weed, red clover and brown snake

As I weighed the possibilities, a slender head poked out of the opening. Then it hastily withdrew. Cautiously appearing a second time, it was followed by an equally slender neck. Two dark eyes contemplated me a moment; then a delicate tongue flicked out, sampling the air.

I had scooped up a little brown snake, or De Kay's snake (*Storeria dekayi*), about the diameter of a pencil and perhaps half again as long. The snake had found that, by coiling itself into a handful of S curves, it could make itself at home in the old container.

Snakes, along with birds and people and most other animals, don't just wander anywhere. They have a definite territory. To have set that can down in some new location would have amounted to dispossessing the harmless little reptile. So, retracing my steps, I carefully laid the can down in its original spot.

I checked up on the snake a couple of weeks later. It was still there. Apparently its unscheduled tour of the countryside hadn't deterred it from settling down again in the old familiar surroundings.

The little brown snake is at home almost anywhere. Indeed, some books refer to it as the city snake. Often a construction crew, going to work at the site of a new building, will find a city snake or two beneath a pile of lumber. Dispossessed when the land was cleared, the little creature wandered homeless until the new materials arrived. There, from beneath a pile of two-by-fours or a load of concrete block, it sallies forth nightly in search of slugs and earthworms and perhaps an insect or two.

Several other small brownish snakes may share your parks and forests. Many of them are holdovers from the days before their quiet world was scalped and paved and developed. Secretive in habits, they hide under stones and old boards. There they usually escape notice—except by midnight cats and roving dogs and youngsters intent on a little sandlot baseball. Picking up a chunk of wood to use in their game, the kids may discover that first base is already occupied.

Somewhat larger, and much more visible because of their daytime habits, are the striped creatures often called garter or garden snakes. Ranging from one coast to the other and from southern Canada to the subtropics, these members of the genus *Thamnophis* seek only a little shelter and a fair supply of food. They grow up to three feet in length—or more, depending on the species—at the expense of earthworms, frogs, toads, and an occasional mouse or young bird. If their edible neighbors are unwilling to cooperate, garter snakes can subsist on a few insects or spiders, or even an unlucky fish, stranded in a shallow pool.

With few worries as to food or shelter, *Thamnophis* in its dozen or so species has good-naturedly moved over to make room for people. The late great authority on reptiles, Dr. Raymond L. Ditmars, found garter snakes in parks in even the largest cities. A friend and I discovered two of them just outside the visitors' entrance of the huge Coors brewery in Golden, Colorado. Apparently the well-landscaped grounds offered enough privacy so that the peaceful reptiles didn't mind the steady flow of thirsty visitors.

It was a garter snake that pointed out to me one day just how much some creatures have to put up with. After all, if you go back far enough, you find that the native animals are the rightful inhabitants; they were here first. It is *we* who are the intruders, instead of the other way around. And one garter snake, gently insisting on maintaining its birthright, nearly did itself in as a result.

The snake, it seems, lived around the edge of some landscape plantings in Grayling, Michigan. Peg and I were visiting friends there, and we decided to take a stroll around town one afternoon. As we walked past a narrow plant border of a lawn outside a large building, we noticed something unusual taking place beneath a bush. The disturbance was caused by a snake, and it was in a fine predicament. Apparently poking through the leaves and grass clippings and general litter that covered its little domain, the snake had inserted its head through the pull-ring of a pop-top can. Crawling forward, it had inched through the ring as far as the girth of its body would let it go. There the ring stayed. Unable to retreat from its aluminum collar because of the backward pointing scales on its body, the poor snake was in a durned-if-you-do, durned-if-you-don't kind of fix.

We watched for a moment as the unfortunate creature

writhed and twisted and did everything but turn inside out to get rid of its implacable enemy. Then we bent to our task. Gently smoothing the body of the distraught creature, we slimmed it down enough to slide the ring forward over the scales. The snake relaxed completely in our hands while we worked. After the ordeal it lay in my lap as if in gratitude, flexing those aching muscles for a full five minutes. Then it turned and gave us the only farewell a snake knows how to give: a long, infinitely graceful caress across our laps with the entire length of its body. It lowered itself to the ground and faded away through the weeds.

That garter snake made its living on dry, plant-covered ground. Little pools and meandering watercourses may be the home of the more spirited but equally harmless water snake—harmless, that is, unless you're a fish or a frog. Water snakes are accomplished swimmers and excellent divers. They can poke along beneath a bank or through the mud, setting fish, frogs, toads and salamanders off in high gear.

Sometimes you can follow the hidden progress of a water snake by observing the frantic leaps of amphibians; the sudden dashes of fish as they put as much distance as possible between themselves and the snake. I have seen fish skip across the water like a skittering stone, and even jump up on the bank in an effort to leave the entire pond in sole possession of *Natrix*, the swimmer.

The water snake is a strange mixture of shyness and spunk. Too stout to be graceful or swift on land, it seldom strays far from water. It usually drapes itself on a tuft of pond's-edge grass or an overhead limb, so that it can slip to safety at the first hint of danger. Corner it, on the other hand, and it's all fight. It coils and strikes and acts deadly. Like most of our small, nonpoisonous snakes, however, its teeth are meant mainly for holding prey and not as battle weapons. Thus, its bite is about like tearing your hand through a rosebush: unpleasant, but hardly a mortal wound.

Such antics scarcely endear the water snake to people. Add to its portly body a head that flattens into a triangular shape on demand, plus a color pattern that varies from plain muddy to brown-and-yellow diamonds, depending on the species, and you've got a veritable sea serpent. Indeed, when we were kids we used to enter the water with apprehension if anybody reported any "moccasins" about. Nobody was ever attacked, of course; nor would they be.

The true water moccasin is of little concern to anybody more urbanized than a back-country bog trotter. It resembles the nonpoisonous water snake, yes, in both looks and action. However, it prefers Southern waters; and the fewer people, the better. At one time the moccasin did, indeed, wander into the ditches and streams of towns south of the Mason-Dixon line. Such rash actions usually triggered a posse that stopped short of nothing but annihilation of the offending reptile.

The same can be said of copperheads and rattlesnakes. They have long since learned to stay clear of anything that smacks of civilization, too.

Occasionally, a rattler-that-isn't turns up in some suburban back yard. This is the checkered adder (*Lampropeltis doliata*). Given its common name because of a pattern of black-edged reddish blotches on a light background, this snake sometimes vibrates its tail when aroused. If the tail happens to be resting in some dry leaves, there's your "rattler."

Nor does the snake's behavior inspire confidence. Although it flees from your presence when possible, it defends itself fiercely if you're so rash as to corner it. And there, as you stare apprehensively at the coiled and striking creature, you suddenly realize that one of those red patches covers its nose and forehead—a copperhead, for sure!

The checkered adder is also known as the milk snake. It got this name from its former habit of lurking around barns and outhouses. The farmer thought it was there to steal milk from the cows. Even the most placid bovine, however, would scarcely stand for this type of nonsense from such a needle-toothed critter. But a good story dies hard, and many a "milk snake" has been sent to eternity because its constant search for rats and mice brought it right to the place where it was most needed.

Today the milk snake can still be found where livestock and grain provide easy living for rodents. The snake is a better ratter than any cat, as it can follow its prey right down into a hole. Gifted with an ability to climb, it also searches trees and bushes for young squirrels, birds and their fledglings. Add to these an occasional frog, lizard or earthworm and you can see why this relative of the somewhat more rural king snake finds that food is no problem—if it can only remain hidden between meals.

In marked contrast to the peppery milk snake are the two gentle green snakes. *Opheodrys aestivus* may be about three feet long. It bears scales that are keeled, or ridged along their midlines. O. *vernalis* is smooth and satiny, and usually less than two feet long. Colored to match the green of the grass and bushes, these inoffensive creatures are often known simply as grass snakes. They scout the foliage for caterpillars and other insects, easing along so slowly that they're hardly noticed even when in motion.

One summery day I was scheduled to do a television show from Broadcast House in downtown Hartford, Connecticut. I arrived early and decided to enjoy a few minutes among the strollers on Constitution Plaza before going inside. As I admired the foliage and developing fruit of a flowering crab apple along the edge of the plaza, a sudden gust of wind shook the little tree. Everything swayed but one slender green twig, which instantly stood out because of its immobility.

Curious, I looked more closely. The "twig" was a green snake perhaps fourteen inches long. I had been looking almost directly at it without realizing what I was seeing. For its part, the slender reptile had gazed right back. When the wind blew, I didn't move; and so, neither did the snake. Except, of course, to maintain its position two feet from my nose.

Carefully I raised a hand until the neck was resting on it. Only then did the creature come to life. Flicking its tongue inquiringly, it slowly withdrew, turned gracefully, and vaulted with surprising speed into the upper branches.

When I was on the air an hour or so later I had a wicked desire to tell viewers in my native Nutmeg State about the horrendous man-eater within a couple of blocks of one of New England's busiest intersections. However, I figured that the little snake was living on a precarious edge as it was. All it needed was a few dozen curiosity seekers poking through the wilds of Constitution Plaza on a snake hunt, and the jig would be up for everything that wasn't rooted to the spot.

Perhaps I'd still better caution you, in case you're headed Hartford way. There are plenty of hedges and ornamentals there in that tiny green oasis within the concrete webwork. Some patch of greenery could yet shelter *Opheodrys*, who may match you stare for stare—and stick its tongue out at you to boot.

That tongue, by the way, is a most marvelous instrument. Far from being the "stinger" that people sometimes believe, it is soft and delicate, like a fine camel's hair brush. Its tip is divided into two slender filaments that are richly endowed with nerves and blood vessels. In fact, the tongue of a snake could almost be said to be a flexible, sensitive nerve. Darting out, the moist tongue "licks" a few particles from the air. These particles may be dust, droplets of water vapor or perspiration, or odors borne in the air itself. Then the tongue transports these particles to a special patch in the roof of the mouth.

Our blunt senses may identify a few odors, but this special set of tissues of the snake's mouth is an unusual chemical laboratory. Known as Jacobson's organ, it exquisitely combines taste and smell so that a fragrance we wouldn't notice at all becomes of great importance.

One small garter snake I took with me on my lectures gave a startling example of just how keen this combined smell-taste of a snake may be. Susie was a friendly little snake, with about fifty lectures to her credit. She had been petted by hundreds of school children and admired at a respectful distance by hundreds more. Those for whom the touch of Susie was their first such contact with a snake were surprised—and not a little relieved—by the experience. Susie seemed to enjoy it, resting sometimes on three or four hands at once, and obligingly caressing a hand or arm with that delicate tongue.

So it was a complete surprise to me when, as one boy reached for her, Susie darted forward and met him halfway. Then, to my astonishment, she took hold of his thumb. Only it wasn't his thumb at all. The lad, it turned out, was a fancier of snakes himself. The day was rainy, and he had picked up an earthworm on the wet sidewalk. He had meant to see if she was interested in his offering, and she had answered him before he had hardly presented the question. Among all the talk and confusion and grasping hands, she had singled out the one that held the food when it was still about a foot away.

The sense of smell seems to be well developed in most reptiles. Many lizards have a forked tongue similar to that of snakes, and a dead fish in the water will soon be surrounded by pond turtles. The eyes of reptiles serve them well, too—as you know if you have ever tried to sneak up on a turtle basking in the sun.

Those basking turtles can belong to several species. Like the fish that get dumped here and there to improve the fishing or just because there's nothing else to do with them, turtles may be heisted from somebody's aquarium and slipped into a playground pool when nobody's looking. Or, rescued from the center of a highway and hastily tossed into a car to keep them safe, they ride along as passengers for a while. Then, at some point, the question arises in the rescuer's mind: "But what do I do with it *now*?"

Perhaps that's how the snapper got into that Longmeadow pond. Longmeadow is a quiet suburb of Springfield, Massachusetts, with dignified homes, large lawns, tree-shaded streets and boulevards. One of the main attractions—for me, at least—is a large area that has been set aside for use by humans and wild things alike: the several hundred acres known as Forest Park. There are woodlands in the park, and lawns, and wading pools and playgrounds. There are also several tiny ponds, one of which held a snapping turtle.

It wasn't any ordinary snapper, however. Not unless by "ordinary" you mean about thirty chunky pounds of muscle, fat, leathery skin, moss-covered shell and an irascible temper on a short fuse. The pond was drained one season and in the bottom was the crotchety old chelonian, churning up the mud, and mad at the whole world.

Few people had even suspected the presence of *Chelydra serpentina*—the snaky water monster—in that tiny pond. Children had waded in its shallows for years. Ducks swam on its surface, sometimes with a flotilla of ducklings. One blistering summer day, while our sister Irma kept watch, my brother and I "fell" into its cooling waters. There we gratefully floundered around until an attendant—probably secretly wishing he could join us—appeared from nowhere and chased us.

That chain of ponds was insulated from other bodies of water by a whole city's worth of homes and lawns and streets. Its overflow, however, trickled down through underbrush and swamps and culverts until it joined the Connecticut River a mile away. Perhaps Old Grumpy had navigated the little brook upstream in an earlier day when he was Young Grumpy. Or perhaps he had been scooped off some busy road far away, kept as a curiosity for a while, and finally dumped into that lily pond. At any rate, there he was—to the horror of hundreds of mothers who had pastured their barefooted youngsters in the ripples along the shore.

There had been little danger from the snapper, however. Its incredible temper is apparently mostly a compensation for being caught out of its element. Lacking anything more than a wobbly bit of bony cartilage for a bottom shell, or plastron, it protects its vulnerable self on land by striking out at almost any moving object within reach. This persuades most creatures to remain at an awed distance—which, of course, is the general idea.

In the water, the snapping turtle may be another creature. I have seen a wicked old snapper, lurching out at everything while it was carried by the tail, open-mouthed and menacing, to a nearby pond. Then, the instant it was placed in the water, its whole attitude toward life suddenly changed. Gone was all that bravado: now it tried desperately to escape even while still being held by the tail. Then, when it was let go, it sped into the depths, leaving behind a muddy wake like an underwater bulldozer.

Of course, a bare toe would be as acceptable to those knifelike jaws as would the more prosaic diet of unwary goldfish, bits of hot dogs and waterlogged potato chips. However, a toe doesn't just drift along the bottom all by itself; it's hitched to a laughing, splashing child. It would be a pretty stupid snapper that would not notice such a commotion in the water—and paddle away to the safety of the center of the pond as fast as those webbed feet could take it.

I cannot recall whether more turtles were marooned when that pond went dry or not, but chances are that the pudgy old snapper had company. Pond turtles, or "sliders," as they are sometimes called, may also wander from one body of water to another, whether aided by people or not. Most turtles come out of water now and then; the males apparently for adventure and the females in search of a place to lay their eggs. Then, too, with swamps and ponds being drained and filled, the turtles are forever being forced to move.

Such homeless creatures may follow a stream bed until they come to the welcome expanse of a pond. They may strike out on their own across roads and embankments. If you see such a creature stranded in the middle of the highway be sure to place it in the direction it's headed when you rescue it. It will do little good to place it back where it just came from. The determined creature apparently has difficulty changing its mind. Especially when *you* want it to change.

Since many towns have grown up along rivers, and since the spirit of adventure seems to pervade even these humble creatures, they continue to appear in unusual places. Not long ago, in Annapolis, a diamond-backed terrapin staged a one-terrapin invasion right beneath the noses of the security forces at the entrance to the United States Naval Academy. Apparently something had routed it out of its native brackish swamp. It was discovered by an alert midshipman, who must have broken training long enough to stoop to pick it up. He gave it to us and we released it in a semisalt lagoon on the Virginia shore.

Landlubber turtles may get the wanderlust, too. The common box turtle (*Terrapene* species) may go for a stroll right after a rain. Called forth by the moisture with its promise of newly sprouted mushrooms and tempting worms on the damp earth, the box turtle comes out from beneath the shelter of a log or the roots of an old tree. Ambling about, it appears where no turtles may have been for years. Since it can close its hinged lower plastron tightly against the upper shell like a box—whence its common name—it may survive the ministrations of stray dogs and cats where more fleet-footed creatures wouldn't have a chance.

Then there's the occasional turtle whose presence is the

result of our urge to have something for a pet. Eventually outgrowing the turtle—or vice versa—we relegate it to the nearest pond or park with fond hopes for its well-being. There it languishes for a while, thousands of miles from its native land, sending students of herpetology scuttling for their books.

Nor is such an event limited to turtles, of course. Almost any critter may be taken out on a Sunday afternoon and "given its freedom." I remember a foot-long alligator that Don Brown and I released at Black Rock State Park in Thomaston, Connecticut. We couldn't get it to eat, so we decided to let it make its own way in the world. After we let the toothy creature go at the beach it sank from sight, quite likely forever—which, doubtless, was lucky for the peace of mind of all the swimmers at the park, even though it was hard on the alligator.

One last reptile story. This concerns a creature in its own land—a desert tortoise pictured in an Arizona newspaper a few years ago. Desert tortoises may spend an entire lifetime with no water other than that from succulent cacti and wild fruits and the occasional drenching bonanza of a Southwestern storm.

The tortoise in the newspaper remained in its own native state of Arizona; but it must have been the Christopher Columbus of the chelonians, for it resolutely turned its stumpy little tail on that dry desert. It wandered into a nearby town, and meandered about until it apparently found just what it was seeking.

Hiding beneath a rocky ledge, it snoozed during the heat of day, like any other desert tortoise. But, as soon as the sun began to wane, it came out and began grazing on the sparse greenery of the back yard of its new home. And every few days it made a pilgrimage to its own reptilian version of Shangri-La.

And what was the prize that awaited the adventuresome

reptile? That most precious commodity to be found in desert areas: pure, cool water.

Taking its place by the side of the house, the tortoise eased itself into its private little shower—the heady luxury of five minutes beneath the drip of a window air-conditioner.

7 · *Sing for Your Supper*

"BIRDS. HUNDREDS OF THEM. Millions, even. I can't go out the back door, because it'll scare the sparrows. And the front door is worse—there's a nest in the rosebush."

She looked at me as if somehow all those birds had been in a huge chicken coop and I had been the one to open the door. "Pigeons in the park. Starlings on the soldiers' monument. Feeders and nest boxes all over the place. And every store in town pushing birdseed."

There was a twinkle in her eye, however. "For two cents I'd pull in all the bird feeders and fill the yard full of cats. The only reason I don't do it is that birds are—well, sort of interesting."

And that's it, in a nutshell. Or an eggshell. Birds are, indeed, "sort of interesting." At least that's the official word from an estimated hundred million people in the United States alone, with a proportionate number in Canada. Nearly one person in two feeds the local feathered population, puts up nest boxes, goes on bird walks—or gets dragged into it all by family or friends. The contemplation of this "warm-blooded animal with feathers," as one dictionary puts it, involves more people than any other spectator sport.

Some birders are casual about the whole affair—a few occasional bread crumbs tossed out in the yard, and that's it. Others protest every inch of the way, like my friend whose outburst began this chapter. And a few find in the study of birds enough that is new and refreshing to keep them going a lifetime—like Florence Lynn, of Fortson, Georgia, for instance, who puts out more than two tons of bird food each year.

No matter where you live, there's probably a bird close by. True, they are limited in species and numbers if you are right there in the middle of town, or in a high-rise apartment. But birds are wonderfully motile. A shaggy triangle of grass at a street intersection may become a temporary minirefuge. A windowsill feeder there on the twenty-third floor may give you as much pleasure as that given to Florence Lynn with her three hundred birds a day. Even if you have not a bush or a tree to your name, you may still be able to spy on a bird's nest. Birds, you see, can fly anywhere. And frequently they do.

Take that pigeon in the park, for instance. Known originally as the rock dove, *Columbia livia* has been toted all over the globe by pigeon fanciers. Actually, it probably would have made it here from its native Old World, anyway, for it is a strong flier. It's a born explorer, too, investigating every rooftop, highway bridge and fire escape. It even joins steelworkers as they walk the skeletal girders of a new building. In Western states it has taken up residence in the walls of canyons—a neat little throwback to the rock dove's original habits.

Park managers and people responsible for the general good looks of the town are often unhappy about pigeons. The birds are noisy with their cooing and their loud-flapping wings.

The whitewash of their excrement is an unwelcome addition to the color scheme on the walls of buildings. So the authorities are often chilly toward people who encourage the birds.

Yet for many persons the chance to feed and give help to a wild creature—even if only as wild as a city pigeon—helps fill a need to keep in touch with the distant outdoors.

This scene is doubtless familiar to you. It happened while we were visiting friends in Chicago. Sauntering through a little park, we noted the unusual behavior of the pigeons. As if by a signal, they flew toward an empty bench at the far end of the park. Looking down the sidewalk, we saw the reason for their actions—an elderly couple carrying shopping bags. The shopping bags were bulging with loaves of bread.

Seating themselves on the bench, the man and woman each took out a loaf of bread. Then, to the eager accompaniment of the pigeons, they tossed out handfuls of large crumbs. More pigeons arrived by the second until that elderly couple was hidden from view by a maelstrom of wings and tails and feathers.

The performance lasted about ten minutes. Then, all at once, the close-pressing knot of pigeons fairly exploded. Where before there had been the clamor and cries of the squabbling birds, there was now only the sudden roar of wings. I was almost surprised to find the man and woman still there. Their bags were empty now; they stood up and walked away without a backward glance.

Many cities will lock you up if they catch you feeding the pigeons in such wholesale fashion. The law says it creates a nuisance, or it threatens the public health. However, with such allies as that unknown couple, the birds of Chicago, and hundreds of other cities, will probably stay fat and well-nourished.

You can often find the homes of pigeons if you do a little searching. Their nests are apt to be ramshackle affairs composed of merely a little debris scratched together on a ledge or a flat roof. Two white eggs are the rule. The young, or squabs, are hatched blind, nearly naked and helpless. High above the bustle of the city they cling to their precarious nursery. They grow rapidly on a formula of regurgitated food plus "pigeon milk" produced by special glands in the crops of both parents.

As the squabs get stronger they exercise their wings in the nest, sometimes teetering on the brink of catastrophe. Then, one day, they are off over the city with their parents. Hundreds of feet in the air, their flight had to be right on the first try. There would be no second chance.

One of the pigeon's enemies is that clever buccaneer, the crow. *Corvus brachyrhynchos* seldom nests right in the city. However, it often lives within easy commuting distance. Its home may be in a tall evergreen in the suburbs or the spire of a church. Every dawn it launches forth on its own version of a day's work. An inveterate nest robber, it searches out the eggs and young of other birds. I have watched a crow spear an egg on its bill and then tilt it up so the contents would run down its throat.

On its rascally rounds the crow is usually attended by one agitated small bird after another. Redwing blackbirds gang up on their large relative and drive it away to the edge of their nesting area. Their clamor passes it on to the next pair, and so on, until it runs out of blackbird territory.

The scheming crow often determines just how close it is to a hidden nest by the antics of the smaller birds. If they are only slightly disturbed, it pays them little attention; the nest is not near at hand. However, if they scream and dive at its head the crow may continue until it finds the hidden treasure.

Pigeons have no trees or bushes to conceal the nest, and it is easy picking for the sharp-eyed crow. In his classic *Birds of Massachusetts and Other New England States,* Edward

Howe Forbush told of crows that practically made their living on the pigeons of Boston. Nesting in the trees of the suburbs, the crows merely made leisurely trips into town whenever they got hungry. There they would dine on pigeon eggs or young squab. For their own youngsters they'd find just the right-size squab and bear it back to the nest, trailed by the desperate parents.

Not everything is lost in such forays, however. Obviously the crow has not done away with all the other birds, even though it has had centuries to do its best. If the eggs are taken, the female bird merely produces more, just as a domestic hen may continue her task for nearly a year if each day's egg is removed. And if an ill-concealed nest is destroyed, the birds may learn their lesson and hide the next nest where it will not be found.

This brings up the positive side of the crow's activities. Since crows have been normal—if unwelcome—neighbors of other birds for countless centuries, the threat of their presence keeps the lesser birds on their guard. This has doubtless helped to refine the alertness that we so admire in birds. The slow and incautious, the ones that are sick or careless, seldom live to pass their failings on to the next generation. By aiding in this weeding process, the crow keeps the total numbers of its neighbors down, so there's room for all. The birds that survive are a better breed because of its attentions. Thus, in a way, a predator is the best friend its prey has ever had.

The crow has even worked out a truce with other birds. Around its own nest tree it is quiet and furtive. No nest-robbing here; the ruckus that resulted would call attention to the spot, and perhaps the crow's nest would be discovered. So, in its own bailiwick the big bird is a model neighbor.

The presence of the large crow with its sharp eyes and beak spells caution to other would-be nest robbers. Squirrels are not above taking a clutch of eggs on occasion; neither are raccoons or blue jays. But it may be worth their lives to tinker with a crow's tree. Thus they give the whole area a wide berth. Indeed, a young songbird may live to maturity *because* there's a nest of crows nearby, rather than *in spite* of it.

Many of the crow's habits are repeated on a smaller scale by its cousins, the jays. The blue jay's jaunty crest with its black throat strap, azure back and whitish underparts make it look like a feathered clown. And a trickster it is, but only when the joke is on someone else. Like the crow, it spreads consternation among its smaller neighbors. I have seen a blue jay taking birds out of the nest and dropping them over the side for no apparent reason at all. It also sneaks up on a sleeping cat, pecks at its tail, and leaps tauntingly out of reach of the enraged feline.

Like crows—and like many ruffians whose own habits wouldn't bear too close scrutiny—the jay is quick to spread a self-righteous alarm when some other enemy is about. Let a cat sneak along beneath a hedge, or let a crow or hawk venture near, and the jay screams a warning to the whole neighborhood.

Last winter a trio of jays created a din at the edge of a local school playground. At the top of their lungs they screamed their protest at a creature that lurked near the base of one of the swings. Diving at it again and again they proclaimed the presence of the monster to all the world—a big, fluffy mitten.

In private life *Cyanocitta cristata* is just as secretive as the crow. A pair of jays had a nest in a bushy tree beside our town's general store. Few of the store's patrons suspected the existence of that nest, although it was scarcely thirty feet from the door. True, it was hidden in the leaves, but the jay took pains not to give the secret away. She would land in a tall adjacent shrub whose branches interlaced with the nest tree.

Then, crouching low, she would climb through the branches like some kind of big blue mouse.

When I went to snap her picture, even though it was with a telephoto lens, it didn't take her long to realize that my distant camera was pointed at *her*. As I put my eye to the finder and focused on the nest, I first thought she had flown away. The nest looked empty. Then, as I sharpened the image, I realized that she was still there, but flattened until she was swaybacked on the eggs, with tail and beak pointed straight up in the air. Her strange position changed the outline of the nest. The whole affair looked merely like some wind-tossed twigs that had somehow lodged in the fork of the tree.

Such elaborate precautions allow a blue jay to nest right in your yard, and you never know it is there. With an appetite about as finicky as a garbage-disposal apparatus, it can scrounge a good living. Everything from the scraps in the dog dish to the frozen fruit on your flowering crab apple may serve it well, even if you're the one in every two person's who *doesn't* bother about the birds.

There are other jays too, but they are not so likely to crowd right in on people as the blue jay. Their large black-and-white relatives, the magpies, sometimes remain in a western grove that has been overtaken by the expansion of a town. There they pester the local cats and dogs, helpfully sample the offerings of fruit trees, and abscond with any glittering object from a bottle cap to a pair of eyeglasses.

Distant relatives of the jays, and usually much more welcome as neighbors, are the chickadees, nuthatches and titmice. Gray, black and white is the general color combination of these familiar birds. Along with the common house sparrow, pigeon and blue jay, they are the most frequent visitors to bird feeders. They'll readily occupy a nest box. More about nest boxes, however, in the chapter on how to encourage birds and animals.

Any of the half-dozen species of chickadee can be identified by that dark cap and bib, white face patch, gray body and white underside. There are also refinements like rusty flanks or a brownish head. The real clincher with these chatty, companionable birds, however, is their behavior. Trusting enough to learn to take a seed from your fingers, and agile enough to hang upside down from a doughnut on a string, the chickadees usually make friends wherever they go. The Indians named them after their call, and we still use the name today. While it has been said that if a person knows only three birds one of them will be a crow, I believe another would be the chickadee.

The titmice are less active, but fully as entertaining. A titmouse might be termed a large chickadee with a crest. Whereas the exuberant chickadee will go into a feeder and toss half a dozen sunflower seeds out before it finds just the right one, a titmouse often takes the first seed it finds. Titmice sound a bit like chickadees in their calls, with the addition of a ringing "peter, peter!" They too can hang from a twig at all angles, just like their lively smaller cousins.

For sheer defiance of gravity you'd have to hand it to the nuthatches. You can often see them high in the trees of parks and boulevards, hopping along on the underside of horizontal limbs or descending a tree trunk head first. In fact, these chunky gray and white pixies are often known as upside-down birds—or, as one lady fancier called them, assups. "That name is all one word," she hastened to assure me, "so it's all right."

The term *nuthatch*, by the way, apparently is derived from a common habit of these entertaining little sprites. Seizing a sunflower seed, the white-breasted nuthatch (*Sitta carolinensis*) or one of its three relatives will wedge it in a crack in the bark of a tree. Then, hammering away with its long, sturdy beak, it proceeds to "hatch" the kernel from its shell. When no seeds are available it hatches slumbering insects and spiders from beneath flakes of bark as it travels down the length of a tree trunk.

Incidentally, while the nuthatch inspects a tree mainly from top to bottom, another bird does just the opposite. The tiny brown creeper, smaller than a sparrow, is often found on the same trees as the nuthatches. *Certhia familiaris* flies to the base of one tree and proceeds slowly upward in spiral fashion around the trunk. Reaching the first large limbs, it flies down to another tree and repeats the procedure.

I have seen great trees being worked over from both directions at once by nuthatches and brown creepers. Few hidden insects would be safe from this double attack, no matter which portion of the bark they used for shelter. Better than most sprays or dusts, these living "insecticides" go directly to the source of the woes of the tree. They provide entertainment in the process, too. Besides, they're free.

Tiny and brown, too, are those perky birds, the wrens. Most wrens are about five inches in length—including a sassy tail that is often carried cocked up over the back. Thus they are about half as long as a robin, with perhaps one fourth its bulk.

What they lack in size, however, they make up in spirit. Few birds will face their blistering attack. I've seen a blue jay fleeing headlong with a house wren right tight behind it. Compared to the jay, that wren looked like an agitated bumblebee. The only reason the jay escaped was that it flew out of the wren's territory. Having vanquished its foe, the small bird returned in triumph to the knothole that it called its home.

Almost any garden or park may be blessed by the presence of a house wren. Blessed, that is, if you consider its inroads on the insect population. Not so blessed, perhaps, if other birds wish to use the same cavities for homes. Gifted with boundless zest for house building, the male wren stuffs dozens of twigs into every available nest site. Apparently his idea is to attract a female with his bubbling song and then to give her a choice of already-furnished homes. Or perhaps all the other nests are merely dummies to discourage predators.

Such enthusiasm occasionally spills over where it is not wanted. This wren (*Troglodytes aedon*) is a migratory bird. It arrives fairly late in the spring. Thus it may find a choice nest site already occupied. No matter; it appears with its twigs, anyway. Usually the owners drive it away, but now and again its persistence wins out. Then the eggs and even the young of the original birds are buried in a barrage of little sticks. So perhaps it's lucky that "Jenny wren" destroys great numbers of insects. Its good habits help balance this occasional seamy side of its ledger.

There are seven wrens listed in Roger Tory Peterson's celebrated *Field Guide to the Birds*. Three more are added to the book's Western edition. Most of them stay away from dooryards, with the exception of the loud-singing Carolina wren and the sparrowlike Bewick's wren.

There is one other exception. Peg and I were driving through Phoenix, Arizona, on a balmy April day. We stopped to ask directions at a gas station near the center of the city. As I got out to speak with the attendant, a rich cascade of bell-like notes sounded above the growl of the traffic. Raising my eyes to a tall building I saw the author of this astonishing melody. Its tail jauntily pointing skyward and its white throat swelling with the vibrant song, a canyon wren poured out its refrain from a concrete ledge.

The last time I had heard that song had been in the rugged cliffs of Big Bend National Park in Texas. The canyon wren, however, has learned to make a living in other "canyons"—the imposing concrete ravines of our great Southwestern cities. There it gleans insects and raises its family in some little hollow, high above the street and all but unknown to the throngs below.

Occasionally a wren will join other birds at a feeder, but

usually it prefers an insect diet. The same is true of woodpeckers and flickers. Apparently a feeder offers a change from their search for grubs and similar wood borers.

Sometimes that search for insects runs a woodpecker smack into trouble. Misunderstanding the motives behind their chisel-beaked visitor's antics, people may take a sour view of the appearance of large holes in their trees. Actually, the bird's feeding activity may protect other trees in the vicinity from insect attacks.

These feathered surgeons apparently use, in addition to their keen vision, an acute sense of hearing as they decide when and where to operate. Perhaps, by tapping a likely-looking spot, they can determine whether it has been hollowed out by unseen borers. Then, too, they can probably hear the crunching of tiny but powerful jaws. Even our dull senses will notice the sound if we put an ear against a tree when the insect is at work.

The woodpecker sets to its task, flinging bark and chips until it exposes its prey. Thrusting out a tongue armed with backward-pointing barbs, it extracts the unfortunate borer. Sometimes the excavation takes days, encompasses half the length of a trunk or limb, and may result in the demise of a whole handful of insects.

It may result in the hasty demise of the tree, as well. A woodpecker-weakened limb may fall in a storm. However, it was doubtless going to come down anyway. Woodpeckers seldom drill in sound, healthy wood.

But notice that word "seldom." One of the headaches of utility companies is the uninvited visits of woodpeckers along their power lines. Apparently hearing the humming of wires, the birds are led to search for a teeming city of buzzing insects within the wooden poles. Metal towers get rid of the problem, of course, but they are expensive. Besides, it's easier just to bandage the injured poles.

That's right: bandage. It works, too—at least, sometimes.

On a visit to Sanibel, Florida, we noticed that every so often there would be a piece of cloth wrapped around a utility pole. Inquiring, we found that the bandages helped discourage the explorations of the crow-sized pileated woodpecker. For some reason a flimsy bit of cloth accomplishes what a mouthful of creosoted wood cannot do. Untidy, perhaps, but it cuts down on the phone bills. Or so we are told.

Few woodpeckers have much of a voice beyond a harsh shriek. They often attract attention in another way—by hammering a tattoo on a resounding hollow stub. Some of them find a different drum—a tin roof or a drain spout. Every spring, thousands of loose shingles and clapboards, metal gutters and eaves troughs join the more prosaic dead limbs and decaying trees in proclaiming the sentiments of male woodpeckers all over America. City and country ring to the staccato proclamation: "Here I am—eligible bachelor!"

Then, when a female has come to share his hollow tree trunk, the male is back at the same old bulletin board. Now, however, he rattles out a different message: "Private! Keep off!"

Flickers, those big, brownish woodpeckers, often turn their backs on all that effort involved in carving a living out of insect-riddled trees. They frequently search for easier prey—ants and other insects found along roads and sidewalks. Every autumn I get several telephone calls from people with a roadside casualty—a flicker that didn't give way to a car.

Those roads and streets are home, too, for that hardy import, the house sparrow. Often called the English sparrow, this talkative brown bird came to America via England from probable beginnings in the Mediterranean area. Carefully introduced to New York City in 1852—and a score of cities in subsequent years—it delighted bird lovers with its ability to get along practically beneath the feet of the horses. When the automobile came along, its meals of undigested oats in the droppings of horses began to be in short supply. However, the sparrow was equal to the occasion. It switched to bread crusts, orange peels, gutter gleanings of all kinds.

Spreading from city to city, the prolific sparrow found practically everything to its liking. It can nest almost anywhere, from a hole under the eaves to the ivy on a building. It finds a welcome in the hollow ends of the metal poles of playground swings and in the space between two traffic signs put up back to back on a single post. The dingy brown of the female, the jaunty gray cap and black throat of the male, are known over more than a quarter of the entire civilized world. *Passer domesticus*—the domestic sparrow—fulfills its scientific name well; it is one of the most successful birds of all time.

Another victory must be chalked up to the sparrow's swaggering crony, the European starling. Even though some people had become alarmed by the rate at which the house sparrow was taking over, there were several early attempts to establish starlings in this country. The one that finally "took" was an importation by a New York businessman.

Eugene Scheifflin was a collector. Some people collect stamps; others collect cream pitchers or old campaign buttons. Scheifflin, a student of literature, decided to collect all the birds mentioned in Shakespeare. And so, in 1890, he made the first successful introduction of starlings to New York City.

Apparently the time was ripe. Not only did starlings become established in Central Park, but subsequent introductions in a dozen other cities also proved successful. And before the turn of the century, bird enthusiasts told each other the joyful news all over most of the Eastern seaboard: the starling was here to stay.

Doubtless the garrulous bird with yellow bill and speckled-on-black plumage eventually would have made it to this continent, anyway. Some nursery-rhyme buff, discovering that the blackbirds in "Sing a Song of Sixpence" were most likely starlings, could have decided to import two dozen in a fit of nostalgia. Apparently those four-and-twenty blackbirds made a good pie too, for a hunter's guide of the 1880's encouraged a wider use of starlings as food. "It is a most hearty and delicious foul," the author solemnly assures us.

Even without such accolades, the starling might have come into its own. It is prized as a cage bird in some parts of the Orient because of its vocal powers. A starling can imitate many birds and can even mimic the human voice. It can whistle and chortle, cough and sneeze. When it's in a cage without the distractions of other noises, it builds up an impressive vocal bag of tricks.

A veterinarian friend of mine was called by worried apartment dwellers who wanted suggestions as to how to rescue a kitten. The unfortunate creature was in a huge tree that arched over their street. No, they hadn't seen the kitten, they admitted, but they could hear it crying piteously outside their second-story window. So Don Gill drove around by their house to see what might be done. And you guessed it: their "kitten" turned out to be just a starling.

Any cubbyhole that's large enough may serve as a home for *Sturnus vulgaris.* Starlings nest up under the eaves of houses. They'll occupy a hole in a broken roof. They'll build in the space between two windows if the pane on the outside sash is broken. Sharp-eyed inspectors sometimes can spot construction flaws and hidden gaps by watching where these birds enter the buildings. Although starlings prefer to nest fairly high in the air, they have been known to take up housekeeping in a car that is overparked.

A friend of mine who has a motorboat in Green Bay, Wisconsin, told me that he and his wife started away from the dock one day only to discover they were leaving more of a "wake" than they had planned. A pair of starlings followed them, screaming.

Hastily they returned to shore. On searching, they discovered nearly an armload of grass, feathers and sticks up under the instrument panel. Luckily there were no babies yet; only two of a potential four or five eggs. My friends, hoping the starlings wouldn't mind the translocation, left the whole affair in an abandoned skiff. Then the local supply store made a quick sale: a canvas cover for the motorboat.

Those birds, however, refused to accept the change. They apparently were unable to shift domestic gears. They hung disconsolately around the forbidden motorboat for a day or so, and then took off for more stable quarters.

Incidentally, in spite of the mess it creates around public buildings, plus the noise of its aggregations in trees and parks and its pushy ways toward other birds, the starling does have at least one redeeming feature. In five minutes a flock of starlings can sweep your lawn clean of insects.

Descending with a rush of wings, a flight of the birds will land on the grass. Then they spread out and march forward. A foot or two apart, they stir up chinch bugs, leafhoppers, crickets and Japanese beetles. Like a skirmishing army they cut a swath through the insect population—until, with another rush of wings, they are gone.

Often joining the starlings in their rounds of parks and cemeteries are the redwing blackbirds and their glossy-coated cousins, the grackles. These birds used to be almost entirely swampland residents. However, as civilization has filled in their swamps and put up condominiums where there used to be cattails, the blackbirds and grackles have taken on modern ways, too. A tuft of grass at the edge of an airport or golf course turns out to be as good a spot for a blackbird home as a similar tuft in a marsh. Swampland cedars and other evergreens made traditional grackle homes until we bulldozed them out of sight. However, we obligingly replaced them with spruces and pines. Ornamental shrubs make an acceptable spot for a grackle nest, too.

Cornfields and vegetable gardens supply seed and turned-over worms in the plowing and planting season. Ripening harvest comes along later in the summer. Berries and fruit trees are waiting, too. For the grackles there's the added adventure of pilfering the eggs and young of other birds. As a result of all this food the numbers of redwings, grackles and starlings have burgeoned beyond belief.

Whole counties along their migration routes set up a clamor almost as loud as the birds themselves, as people seek to persuade them to keep moving. Bonfires, shotgun blasts, fake owls, electric wires around buildings, the recorded calls of birds in distress and even rubber snakes have been tried. Most of them soon lose their effect. Frightened from one grove of trees, the thousands of birds settle in another, sometimes breaking limbs from the weight of their numbers.

One evening Peg and I were on the New York Thruway near Albany. Overhead, in the light of the sinking sun, a thin skein of these birds threaded toward the city. The flight was only eight or ten birds wide, but it continued from one horizon to the other. We pulled into a rest area to see how long it was, but we never found out. It was still going when we gave up at dusk. How those late-comers found their way I do not know. Nor do I know what section of the city or its surroundings was favored by their visit.

Sprinkled among the hordes of starlings, blackbirds and grackles during migration may be a species that looks like a cross between a blackbird and a sparrow. The male is greenish-black with a brown head; his mate is a somber dun in color. And well need she bear such nondescript plumage, for she is that parasitic loafer, the cowbird. Her task is to remain as inconspicuous as possible until she can slip an egg into the nest of some smaller bird.

Sometimes the foster-parent-to-be recognizes the unwelcome addition and deserts the nest. Other times she may build another nest right over it. Usually, however, she seems not to notice that the clutch of eggs has increased by a third or a quarter. Settling down, she proceeds to brood over the whole batch.

The cowbird egg, being larger, absorbs and holds more of the female's body heat. Consequently it often hatches first. The young cowbird, thus older and stronger, can raise its hungry mouth higher and wider than its nest-mates. Getting more of the food, it soon overwhelms its foster brothers and sisters. Sometimes it kicks and thrashes and pushes them right out of the nest.

Soon there's nothing left but the young cowbird. Its unsuspecting "mother" labors as hard to feed this one large interloper as she would a whole nestful of her rightful offspring. And so, underneath a rosebush or in a privet hedge, you may see a busy foster parent—a chipping sparrow, say, or some species of warbler—feeding a clamoring youngster almost twice its size.

However, even with such a reprehensible character as the cowbird, not everything is bad. *Molothrus ater*, it is believed, has developed this way of life almost in self-defense. Consider its common name, *cowbird*. This name is taken from its habit of feeding among cattle, sheep and horses. It consumes numbers of insects stirred up in the grass as they graze. Thus its food habits can scarcely be condemned.

Before we came along with our domestic herds, the cowbird consorted with the bison, or buffalo. These great wild animals had no fences to confine them, but sometimes traveled more than thirty miles a day. For a female cowbird to remain with such restless companions and attempt to maintain a home at the same time was out of the question. So she pressed other birds to act as surrogate mothers.

Whether that's exactly how it started or not, nobody knows. However, the baby-sitting scheme has worked so well that today every cowbird is a foster child. And so it will continue

—even though its wandering herds of "bison" have shrunk to a pony in a paddock or somebody's pet goat tied out in the back yard.

Your all-city sanctuary includes other avian visitors that have learned to get along on second best, so to speak. Some of them are doing very well, indeed. Robins have thousands of acres of golf courses and cemetery lawns for their pursuit of the lowly worm. For dessert they can choose the fruit of delicacies like cherries, pears and a hundred ornamental shrubs. The wood thrush finds such a good living in thousands of suburban back yards that some books offer it a new nickname; this speckled brown bird with the incredibly beautiful flutelike notes, they say, should be called the city thrush.

The gentle bluebird may gladden your heart with its liquid warble and incredibly blue coat. Although it cannot stand the competition of city life, this azure-colored thrush may take up residence in a suburban nest box. More about bluebirds, by the way, in the "Welcome Mat" chapter.

The mockingbird gets along with people, too. The gray bird with white breast and flashy white patches in the wings may be lured by handouts at a feeder in all but the most persistently paved and solidly cemented portions of the city. It has an astonishing repertoire, repeating the songs of many of the birds you know—and many that *nobody* knows. Listening, you can understand well its scientific name—*Mimus polyglottos*, the mimic of many tongues.

There are two birds for whom smoke and concrete pose no problem at all. These are the nighthawk and the chimney swift. Both used to call the open country their home. Now they reap the bonanza of all those insects around and above man's habitations.

The nighthawk (*Chordeiles minor*) is a robin-sized gray bird with white patches on its underwings. It flies with strong wingbeats over cities, dodging and turning the feasting on the thousands of moths and beetles and flies attracted by the bright lights.

One night Peg and I went to a drive-in theater. The insects were out by the hundreds, and soon there were three nighthawks zooming and diving through the beam of light of the movie. Their gyrations made weird shadows on the screen. Their loud nasal calls, sounding like a Bronx cheer, scarcely added to the movie's tender love scene, either.

Finally, after much blowing of horns, the operator realized what was wrong. The soul of resourcefulness, he switched off the projector, turned on the dim lights at the snack bar and announced an intermission. The feathered gate-crashers, deprived of *their* refreshments, sought better pickings elsewhere.

Nighthawks once nested in the sparse grit on ledges and rocky outcrops. With the development of gravel-roofed buildings, here were "ledges" made to order. No raccoons or opossums or other climbing animals came to bother them, either. And so it is entirely possible that your office building may display the two mottled eggs of a nighthawk up there in plain sight on its pebbly roof.

The nighthawk's distant cousins, the chimney swifts, have been called "flying cigars." Their body is about the size and shape of a half-burned stogie. Long wings beat with a rapid motion, emphasizing the staccato of their chittering calls. Like the nighthawks they often fly right over the most densely populated cities in search of insects. They fly by day, however—almost constantly, from dawn until dusk.

At one time chimney swifts nested in hollow trees and caves. John James Audubon managed to crawl inside such a tree while the swifts were resting overnight during migration. He estimated that the interior held nine thousand of the sooty-colored birds.

When people came along and erected brick chimneys all

over the landscape, the swifts moved right in. Heat and smoke were a minor problem—after all, many chimneys are unused during the summer. Plastering twigs to the inside of the chimney with their abundant and gluey saliva, the swifts make a saucerlike nest. Indeed, the famous birds'-nest soup of China is concocted from the sticky saliva of one of the swift's Asiatic cousins.

When I taught at a small college in Farmingdale, on Long Island, about thirty miles out of New York City, we used to watch the swifts enter the chimney of the heating plant. Idle for the summer, the plant's great smokestack became the center of a vortex of hundreds of swifts each evening. They would swirl in a descending spiral until each was swallowed in turn, as if by a huge, silent vacuum cleaner.

Accomplished fliers too are those slender, graceful birds known as swallows. If you have a garage or tool shed you may find yourself host to a pair of barn swallows. They build in inside corners where wall and roof meet, or up under the shelter of an open porch.

One high-school commencement I attended took place in the city park. The platform for the dignitaries was on the steps of the town hall, which fronted on the green. All through the ceremony the barn swallows circled and fed their young in a nest on top of one of the fluted pillars. Their manners were impeccable; not one of the somber-gowned figures beneath them collected a single unwanted souvenir.

The barn swallow has a blue-black back, reddish underparts and deeply forked tail. The closely related tree swallow is metallic blue-green on top, white below, with a tail only slightly notched. Tree swallows were named because of their habit of building in hollow trees and knotholes, but they have readily turned to nest boxes when such refinements are available. A multiple dwelling of several compartments on a high post may be used by that large swallow, the purple martin. (Suggestions for homes for these birds will be found on pages 230-35.)

Cliff swallows plaster little gobs of mud up under the eaves of buildings until they have made a bottle-shaped nest. They will also build under structures like the Brooklyn Bridge, for instance, which will often hold a regular avian zoo of pigeons, swallows, sparrows and starlings. Bank swallows used to build in riverbanks. Now they also make nest holes in the falls of gravel pits. Sometimes the babies tumble to their death as a new construction project calls for more sand.

Various small birds—the song sparrow, for instance, and the goldfinch, or wild canary—often nest where there's just a spare bush or two. Orioles build their graceful hammocks in the tallest trees overhanging Main Street. Vireos inspect those same trees for insects. Tiny hummingbirds may visit the flowers—especially the red ones; so strongly does the color attract them that they may try to get nectar from the little red reflector signs along private driveways.

Half a hundred species of wood warblers may pass through almost any city park on migration. Feathered tourists on vacation, they arrive just in time for a smorgasbord of thousands of newly hatched insects in the tender spring foliage.

The warblers return in autumn from Northern breeding areas, but they are seldom noticed. Their colors are more somber at that time. They are quieter, too, with little of the excitement of song that attended their spring migration. So they are still like tourists—at the end of the holiday, soberly going home.

All those birds around the buildings and lawns represent more than lovely voices and pretty colors, however. Hawks and owls have to live, too. A flock of pigeons under a bridge may be the unwilling target of a marauding owl. A bird at a feeder may find itself the main item of fare for a hawk or even a shrike.

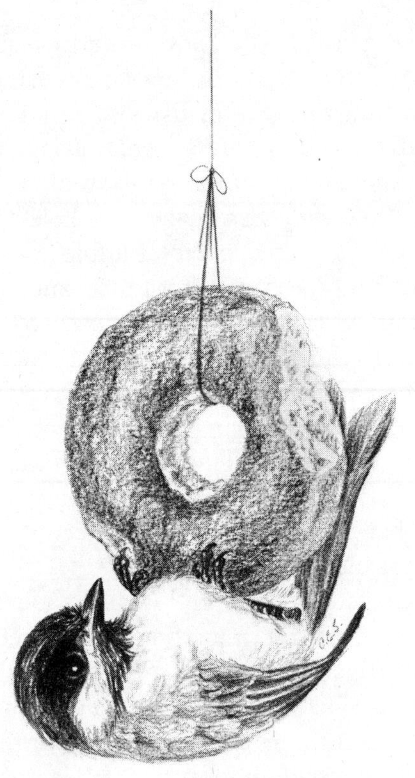

Chickadee

Shrikes ordinarily tend to stay in the country. However, they, too, have learned to change with the times. If you see a gray-and-white robin-sized bird with a black mask, chances are that it's a shrike. You can be sure of it by noting the actions of the other birds—or, rather, by noting the *lack* of action; each bird freezes to the spot the minute the shrike appears.

The nuthatch hangs motionless on the underside of its limb. The chickadee stops so suddenly that it holds the sunflower seed forgotten in its beak. Even the blue jay, which should be large enough to have no fear, stands like a statue.

The shrike, having zoomed to a perch atop the highest tree, surveys the tableau beneath it. The smaller birds scarcely blink. After a few moments, down plummets the shrike. If the other birds keep their self-control, they remain as if cast in bronze. But let one bird stir and the shike is after it.

Away they go, pursuer and pursued. The stark scene relaxes. Cardinals again flaunt their scarlet plumage. Evening grosbeaks in yellow, black and white go back to shelling out sunflower seeds—a cup a day for a dozen birds, if you permit them that much. Other birds drift down from the trees and bushes. Soon the yard is as it was before.

If the predator is a hawk, the strike is quicker. Low-flying, hedge-hopping hawks known as *accipiters* come in at treetop level. Their short, rounded wings provide bursts of speed, while their long tails allow sharp turns in pursuit of fleeing prey. Scattering the smaller birds in a panic, they single out one and try to overtake it before it can flee into a bush.

Accipiters are in several sizes. The crow-sized Cooper's hawk and its somewhat larger cousin, the goshawk, are woodland birds, so you can probably dismiss them here. The smaller sharp-shinned hawk, however, often visits built-up areas and may terrorize a yardful of birds for several days before its wanderlust takes over. It is a couple of inches longer than a robin—the "sharpie" being about a foot long—and is colored like most accipiters with a blue-gray back, barred breast and banded tail.

More leisurely flights are the rule with those circling, soaring hawks known as *buteos*. Seeking an updraft like a sailplane, a red-tailed hawk, or a rough-leg, or one of a dozen other buteos may cruise high over a town or city. However, it is scouting for mice, rats or rabbits, not small birds. Its broad wings and wide tail are meant for soaring, not pursuing its agile feathered neighbors.

The small birds are aware of its limitations, too. Beyond an occasional glance in its direction—as if to keep everything honest—they pay the buteo little heed. In fact, you can often tell what general type of hawk you are seeing by watching the actions of other birds. If they are only mildly concerned, it's probably a buteo. If they scream and act panicky it's more likely an accipiter.

Swift as an accipiter, but listed with the birds known as falcons, is the little sparrow hawk. Like the other falcons it has long, pointed wings and a long tail. Europeans know it as the *kestrel*: a better term than sparrow hawk, since its normal food is not sparrows at all. It *looks* like a sparrow in having a rust-colored back and streaked breast; hence the name. But it feeds on mice, grasshoppers and crickets, plus an occasional snake or small frog.

Look for the sparrow hawk on wires along streets and highways. It may appear like a large robin, but the hawklike beak gives it away. Its flight is bolder and swifter than that of a robin, too. A sparrow hawk may hover on beating wings over a field or meadow, peering at the ground beneath. Then, with a downward swoop, the little falcon pounces on some insect or rodent.

The much larger peregrine falcon, or duck hawk, once chose the tops of tall buildings as a favorite perch. From there it would dive among the pigeons like a feathered rocket. Often it would strike its prey with a clenched fist as it hurtled by. The pigeon would seemingly explode in a burst of feathers. It would be dead before it hit the earth.

Today the peregrine falcon is gone from all but a few wilderness cliffs. The pigeons still have their problems, however. The great horned owl nests in broken trees, under bridges and in old buildings. From here it's an easy flight to the nearest pigeon roost.

Another feathered nemesis may put in an appearance every

few years. One January day Peg and I were driving along a road on the edge of Schenectady, New York. Suddenly Peg chuckled. "What kind of a sign was *that*?" she asked.

I shrugged. "Didn't see any sign, Peg."

She was thoughtful a moment. Then she turned and looked out the back window. "Good heavens, it's still there. Stop. Turn around!"

So we retraced our route. Now I saw it, too—a large white blob, perhaps two feet tall, on a traffic marker that hung over the street. Sitting there, looking as if it had just flown out of a billboard advertisement for cigars, was that sporadic visitor from the frozen north, a great white owl.

Why *Nyctea nyctea* leaves the tundra every few years is not known. Some biologists feel that a periodic shortage of arctic lemmings may cause it to seek a living elsewhere. However, the appearance of the owl does not necessarily correspond to a lean year in the number of these Northern rodents. Other biologists think the pressures of its own population might force the owl to leave home. But why go hundreds of miles?

There may be other factors, too. At any rate, there the owls are, every few years. As recently as last winter one sat for two weeks above the clock on the steeple of the Unitarian Church in the heart of Burlington, Vermont. It remained there, motionless, most of the day, except for periodic flights right down Church Street. As it flew, it spread pandemonium among pigeons and starlings and sparrows.

For ten or fifteen minutes after such a flight, the whole street would be swept clean of the frightened birds. Then, slowly, they would drift back into sight. There they would feed, keeping nervous watch of the apparition that sat there like a great white statue.

A barn owl in an old building, its eyes solemn in a heart-shaped face, may welcome sparrows and starlings as a spider welcomes a fly. However, the barn owl and its smaller relative, the eight-inch screech owl, usually stick to a diet of mice and rats.

Almost any hawk or owl, by the way, will take rodents when possible. After all, these are wild creatures. They will seize any opportunity that comes along, whether it wears fur or feathers. I remember once lamenting to my mother when I was a child after I had seen a sparrow hawk swoop down and carry off a goldfinch. "But the book says they don't catch other birds!" I wailed.

"That's right," Mother gently agreed. "But I guess the sparrow hawk hasn't read the book."

While the back yards and bridges and buildings may sport their crops of birds, the ponds and pools and puddles also have their share. Since most cities are built on a river or ocean front, water birds may be anywhere. They join you at the beach, at the wading pool, and even at the river that flows through the center of town.

Indeed, it was at the mouth of such a river that a most unusual bird sighting was made. The sea gulls that inhabit such places are generally gray and white, with perhaps a bit of color on beak or legs. A small, pinkish gull in the Boston area attracted bird enthusiasts from hundreds of miles away. People traveled all weekend to add it to their life lists, and whole bus tours were organized just to see this one particular bird—the rare, graceful Ross's gull.

The sighting of that gull, unusual as it was, could hardly eclipse an event in the lives of Miller and Margaret Stewart, of Toronto. They tell about it in their delightful book *Bright World Around Us* (Pocket Books, 1971). Early in their days as birders they approached the great naturalist Dr. W. E. Saunders with reports of an unusual gull they had seen around the river near Windsor, Ontario. It was the regulation gray and white they told him, but with rosy head and sides.

Dr. Saunders shook his head. He was familiar with the

gulls of the region; there was definitely no such bird. But they insisted, and he went to see for himself. He found the bird, all right—several of them. They were swimming around in the river below a chemical plant. Dabbling in the water, the gulls ducked their heads and bodies in the plant's floating wastes—and came up a beautiful blushing pink.

Except for such developments, the Northeastern gulls you'll see around cities will probably be common herring gulls or the slightly smaller ringbills. These will have gray backs, with white heads and tails. Westerners will see the similar California gull. Along the shore you'll find the laughing gull and Bonaparte's gull, both with dark heads, gray backs and white tails. Bonaparte's gull is the smaller, with whitish tips to the wings.

Winter plumage of gulls, plus that of their young, may create a bird that looks like anything from an all-white dove to a gigantic sparrow. Many a seasoned ornithologist has hastily reached for the bird book in trying to identify immature gulls or those out of season.

Gulls have solved the problem of people in many ways. They use pilings and buildings for perches. By the thousands, they visit garbage dumps. A dump outside Manchester, New Hampshire, harbors so many gulls that their screams drown out your car radio as you drive past on Interstate 89. And the upwelling sewage in the bay near Danvers, Salem and Ipswich, Massachusetts, is the center of a constant cloud of the wheeling, screaming, diving birds.

Gulls often follow the farmer's tractor as it exposes worms and insects. Sometimes they alight on the tractor itself. They will visit little home gardens, too. In the Northeast and Far West such gulls are usually ringbills; you can spot them by a dark "ring" of pigment that seems to encircle the beak near its tip. In Mid-Atlantic states the gardener's companions are more likely the black-headed laughing gulls.

It seems ridiculous to see these paddle-footed birds treading the soil perhaps miles from water. To them, however, there's nothing strange in it at all; they don't know that they are listed as water birds. Like my sparrow hawk of years ago, they haven't read the book.

Another bird that would seem more at home at the shore is the common killdeer. It is one of the plovers, a group often found at the water's edge. Two black necklaces cross the white breast of this strong-flying bird with the reddish rump and loud, ringing voice—"Kil-dee! Kil-dee!" In fact, so garrulous is the killdeer that its vocal prowess is carried over into part of its scientific name—*Charadrius vociferus*.

The killdeer seems to delight in putting its nest where it is right in the way. One half of the circular access road to a friend's estate in Smithtown, Long Island, was closed off for two weeks while a killdeer sat on her eggs in the middle of the driveway. A whole corner of a drive-in theater near Scranton was marked off limits, according to a newspaper report; about two dozen of its parking places were left vacant because of the insistent protests of a killdeer.

The best little bit of chicanery, however, is taking place right here in my own little town as I type these words. A female killdeer has claimed a spot out beyond second base at the local baseball field. Whenever a player ventures near, the female goes into her wounded-bird act. Her "broken" wing dragging, voice crying piteously, she kicks up the dust in her death struggle as she attempts to lure the intruder away from her four speckled eggs.

The Reverend Sam Cofone, whose church ball team owns the playing field, put logs and boards in a large circle all around the killdeer's nest. Then the team set up a special ground rule. If a fly ball lands in that charmed circle, the batter is automatically out.

Other shore birds may visit ponds, little and big. One may

be a gangling heron, whose stilt legs allow it to walk the muddy shallows in search of frogs, fish and tadpoles. Another may be a spotted sandpiper, scarely larger than a sparrow, whose speckled body is forever teetering on its slender legs as if it were in imminent danger of losing its balance. In between are half a hundred other waders, muddiers-of-water, liers-in-wait, stalkers and striders dedicated to the proposition that not all methods of gaining a living from the water are created equal.

One bird shuffles through the mud and snaps up the disturbed worms and insects before they can disappear again. Another stirs the same water—and spears the little fish that come to the feast. One uses an outspread wing as a sunshade so that it can look down into the depths; another stands motionless, until some incautious fish rises to the surface. Still others probe the wet sand and mud for worms and crustaceans.

The little flocks of sanderlings (*Crocethia alba*) run up and down the beaches of the entire world, just ahead of an approaching wave and back down as it recedes. Poking busily with their little black beaks, they capture beach organisms that are tumbled about by the current. In contrast, the woodcock (*Philohela minor*) walks slowly through many a muddy field at dusk, treading with a peculiar little dance. The dance jars the ground and brings earthworms to the surface—as if to see if it really *is* raining.

Water is the chosen environment of our last group of birds. These are the ducks, geese and swans. Mute swans (*Cygnus olor*), brought over from Europe, are the common orange-billed swans familiar to most of us. They have turned their backs on the formal pools where they began, and now grace many a little park all over the world. A white swan with a black bill is the whistling swan (*C. columbianus*), but you'll see it more in bays and open water.

Many a city lake has its real, live Canada geese. Gifted

with remarkable resiliency, *Branta canadensis* can desert its wilderness haunts. Taking up civilized life it can sozzle through mud like a puddle duck, picking up bread crusts and making a fine living right there among the rental canoes and sailboats. Its long, cackling flight lines arranged in a V high in the air are a familiar sight over much of North America in spring and fall.

While there are several sizes and colors of ducks on those puddles in the park, chances are many of them trace back to the mallard (*Anas platyrhynchos*). Its breeding powers border on the phenomenal—at least when it comes to successful mating with other ducks. A mallard can cross with wild or domestic birds almost at will.

Its blend with the familiar white Pekin, for instance, may present the world with tan, white or tricolored offspring. They may be speckled brown like a female mallard or may bear the familiar green head, gray body and curled tail feathers of the drake. White wings, piebald body, the female's loud quack or the drake's soft *quish-quish* may be scattered through those youngsters. There is as much variety among them as among canines at a home for wayward dogs.

Mallards themselves may set up a nest in some marshy corner of the pond. The female pulls downy feathers from her breast as a soft mattress for the eggs. Sometimes she places some of the down, plus leaves, on her back. Then, as she noiselessly departs the nest the down slides from her body and forms an insulating, camouflaged coverlet for the eggs.

Mallards breed with the wild black duck, too. The black is like its name: both males and females are dark in color. About the only relief to the somber streaks on a lighter background is the blue speculum, or flight patch, in the wings. Blacks seldom visit ponds where there are many people, however; they are much too shy.

An occasional teal may alight on the water for a day or so.

Once in a while you may see the wood duck with its glossy crest and rainbow of colors. But, mostly, the ducks in the little civilized ponds are mallards, or half-mallards—or, of course, somebody's pets gone native. If you're fortunate enough to be on a larger body of water—in Cleveland, say, on Lake Erie, or in my own Burlington on Lake Champlain—your web-footed neighbors may be counted in the hundreds.

And there they are—those birds by the hundreds, as my friend said at the beginning of this chapter. I guess what makes them so interesting to many people is the number of ways you can get to know them—their songs, their colors, their habits, even their silhouettes. Then, too, they flit around so much you're never sure what you might see next.

That friend who complained about birds, by the way, lives in Pittsburgh, Pennsylvania. Her name is Beatrice Dye. And the sparrows do, indeed, monopolize the back yard. Every year there is some kind of nest in the bushes or birdhouse by the front door too. But Sam Dye is an understanding husband. And, luckily, he's handy with hammer and saw.

Knowing how his wife would like to have at least *one* undisturbed entrance to the house, he cut a new doorway in the east wall. They needed a garage, anyway, so he added one. During nesting season you enter the garage, turn right at the power mower, and go up the steps to the kitchen.

But now there's another problem. Beatrice just told me about it in a letter. A pair of phoebes have begun to build a nest over *that* door too.

Carrye E. Schenk

8 · Possum in the Parking Lot

THEY STOOD THERE by the car's front wheel, in the center of a ring of people. "What do you suppose they are?" somebody asked.

"Beats me," said somebody else. "But they got a face like Porky Pig—"

"—and a tail like Mickey Mouse," added another voice.

Curious, we edged through the crowd. It was late dusk, there on Long Island's south shore. A perfect time for almost any critter to be moving around, I figured.

Finally we got close enough to see what they were talking about. Half hidden by the wheel, but just as curious about us as we were about them, were four half-grown opossums. Their faces showed white in the beam of someone's flashlight. We could see their shell-thin ears, dark eyes, and inquisitive snouts. Come to think of it, those snouts with their naked nostrils *did* look as if they belonged on some kind of long-nosed pig.

One of them reached forward with a hind foot to scratch

its shoulder. The foot had long, fingerlike toes and a short, projecting "thumb." Someone laughed. "Look! It's got hands on its feet!"

The animal that scratched itself moved a bit away from the others. Now we could get a good view of its whole body. "Possum!" a child cried. "It's a possum! There's one in our school book."

"Naw," said his friend scornfully. "It's an *o*-possum. Say it right."

The first child had a ready answer. "All right—*o*-possums. But why ain't they dead? When they get scared they play dead, the book says."

As if to test whether the book was correct, someone tossed a wad of paper in the direction of the four animals. The effect was instantaneous. Not on the opossums, but on the people.

The opossums merely retired into the darkness under the car. Now they were hidden, and this, of course, made them seem dangerous. Then one ran over and hid beneath a neighboring car. Somebody gasped, and the crowd shrank back—way back.

"Here they come!" yelped a voice. The flashlight gyrated in a new direction. People melted away from its beam as if it were a fire hose. In an instant the whole crowd fled.

"Hold it!" yelled someone else. "Possums won't hurt you!"

"They won't *catch* me!" was the retort.

And so, there in the Massapequa Shopping Plaza, half an armful of kitten-sized opossums vanquished half a hundred full-sized people. And they did it, not by playing dead, but by seeming to be very much alive. Indeed, human imagination had made these poke-along creatures more alive and agile than they would ever be in their whole lifetimes.

My son and I waited until there were only a few hardy

souls left. One was the man with the flashlight. Adding the beam of our own light to his, Tom and I studied the little creatures. With most of the crowd gone, the opossums had ventured out from beneath the car. One of them climbed partly up on the back of another for a better look. Its front paws were like hands, too, each with five little fingers. Its grizzled-gray coat and white-furred face made it seem infinitely old.

In a sense, it *was* old. Although this little creature had been on earth only about three months, it claimed a venerable lineage. For the opossum is the sole surviving North American member of one of the world's oldest mammalian families. This family, the marsupials, or pouched mammals, stretches back in an unbroken line to the days of the dinosaurs. Running around beneath the feet of these great lords of the earth, the newly arrived mammals may have seemed insignificant. However, scientists believe they quite likely fed on the eggs of the gigantic reptiles, and thus helped speed the destruction of the big creatures.

Now, some 150 million years later, four more marsupials crouched at the feet of modern lords of the same earth. Woolly mammoths, twelve-foot-high bears and saber-tooth tigers have flourished and died, but the marsupials have kept right on through it all.

True, they have disappeared from many parts of the world where the competition is fierce. Australasia contains the bulk of them today where there's a biologically slower pace. But the dim-witted plodding opossum still manages to survive right here in hurry-up America. Indeed *Didelphis marsupialis* is ranging wider all the time. In Grandpa's day it was native to the Southern states; now it explores garbage pails, extinct picnic fireplaces and curbside debris all the way into Canada.

What gives the opossum such an edge over its speedier and smarter neighbors? Doubtless that marsupium, or maternal pocket, is a big help. Borne by all the opossum's relatives, from some tiny mouselike creatures to the great gray kangaroo, it's a warm, safe cradle and nursery. Each grublike opossum baby attaches to a teat in the marsupium and remains there about six weeks. Then it continues to travel with its mother until able to care for itself.

The feat of "playing 'possum" is a hard act to follow, too. An opossum, attacked by a dog or cat, falls as if dead. Even if its enemy shakes and bites it, the opossum remains limp as an old sock. Such lack of cooperation on the part of its prey soon discourages the predator. It loses interest and walks away.

After a few minutes the durable critter comes back to life. Shaking itself, it shambles off to the nearest tree or hollow log. Chewed and limping it may be, yes—but it is still alive and reasonably well. Score one more for the opossum.

The opossum can also thrive on almost anything it finds in the line of food. Apparently if something can be chewed, it's worth a try. When I worked at the Patuxent Research Refuge in Maryland, we analyzed the contents of the innards of several hundred opossums taken by hunters. There were the usual fruits, berries and insects—plus such delicacies as pieces of popsicle sticks; bits of paper cups; cork liners from the inside of bottle caps; rubber bands. There was a shred of newspaper headline that read "First"—although we were sure it wasn't!

There was also an interesting item that would have been ominous if we had been inquiring into the ways of a lion, say, or a tiger. In an opossum, however, it just made us grin and wonder—a genuine, lifetime-point, well-chewed half of a Waterman's fountain pen.

So, perhaps, in the presence of such man-eaters, those panicky shoppers in the Massapequa Mall did well to quit the premises, after all.

Actually, however, it was a mystery as to what the four little opossums were doing without their mother. Perhaps she had been hit by a car. Perhaps she had tried to run or fight, instead of surrendering. Opossums don't always play dead, by any means; so, she might have been bested in combat. Or possibly she had just turned her back on her family. At any rate, the youngsters were definitely on their own. But a parking lot, we figured, was not the best place for them, so Tom and I shooed the little quartet off into the greenery.

They scrambled into the bushes—probably to reappear as soon as our backs were turned. After all, that parking lot held plenty of inviting tidbits. If their luck held, they would have four or five years ahead of them to explore everything from trash cans to bird feeders. Or, as happened once with friends in Flushing Meadow, New York, they might appear as an unscheduled attraction at a garden party.

If "phlegmatic" can describe easy-going old Br'er 'Possum, "frantic" describes his tiny neighbor, the shrew. Everything a shrew does is at top speed. It scampers about on twinkling feet through the runways of mice, setting the little rodents off in a panic. It nips a beetle here, an earthworm there. Catch it and it's so high-strung it may faint in your hands.

Shrews are fearless little creatures. They'll go almost anywhere. Few enemies are too formidable—either in their own size or, if the shrew is riled enough, in any size at all. One summer day I watched a cat stalking mice in a field. It sneaked up on a tuft of grass, every nerve alert. Twitching its tail, it gathered itself, pounced—and pounced back.

The "mouse" it had meant to catch turned out to be a shrew. Apparently missing its leap, the cat had merely startled the tiny creature. Enraged, the shrew launched a chattering counterattack. I could see it, no bigger than my thumb, as it ran right up to the top of the tuft of grass. Then, before the cat could strike again, its intended prey vanished—doubtless still hurling curses at its gigantic enemy.

Biologically speaking, shrews date even farther back into the dinosaur days than the opossum. For ages they wandered the earth, feeding on insects, crustaceans and other animals. Most of the living shrews are found in warmer parts of the globe: their high rate of metabolism hardly permits them to cope with winter's cold and hunger. However, a couple of species have pursued their insects and snails and millipedes right into the wilds of our parks and playgrounds. There they'll scramble out their high-speed little lives at the expense of almost anything that's edible—including mice and other shrews, if they're slow to get out of the way.

You can tell a shrew from a mouse by the way it looks and the way it acts. It appears to be a half-sized "mouse" with a pointed snout, almost uniformly gray fur and no apparent eyes or ears. In action it may run everywhere at once, reversing and changing direction like a character in a speeded-up movie. Sometimes it carries on a continual conversation with itself, uttering a series of tiny squeaks that tumble out so fast the shrew sounds like a leaky radiator.

We played host to a shrew once. We were living in a house with a hole in the floor where a water pipe had been removed. We knew exactly when the shrew entered our home for the first time; there was a commotion in the walls as it routed every mouse in the place. Then for several days we could hear it buzzing to itself as it cleaned up the insect population.

Finally it discovered the hole in the floor. From then on it paid nightly visits to the dog dish to finish up the scraps that Jack didn't touch. It stayed with us all winter, perhaps bearing a litter of shrewlets in the process—although, understandably, we never saw the babies. Sociability is not the shrew's strongest asset, and after the youngsters have traveled with their mother a couple of weeks a gigantic free-for-all sends them off in separate directions.

Related to the shrews—and, like them, classified as Insectivores because of sharp-pointed, unspecialized teeth that are just the thing for eating insects—are those subsurface engineers, the moles. Almost any lawn, garden or golf course may harbor a mole or two, often in spite of our efforts to the contrary. The ridges and piles of earth helpfully poked up by moles make them less than welcome wherever they appear.

Actually, the mole's activities are mainly to the good, even if in the process it causes you to miss a putt or lose half a row of dahlias. It seems that the mole is really interested in small edible neighbors in the soil around it—the earthworms and insects that share its cool, dark world. Those mounds and runways and pyramids merely mark its progress.

It's the camp followers, so to speak, that help bring the wrath of the householder down on moles. If a mole burrows alongside a line of vegetables or flowers it's usually because of the worms and insects that enjoy the fertile soil and the tasty roots. Then, after the mole has pioneered the way, mice and other rodents bring up the rear. As they go, they help themselves to the roots that have been exposed. The end result is the same as if the mole had attacked the crops in the first place.

Moles, admittedly, add little to the aesthetic value of a lawn. But, for what it's worth, you'll seldom find a mole in poor soil. So, I suppose, you can take heart as your lawnmower scalps the molehills and tosses gravel all through the grass; you've got a potentially good lawn there.

There are three common species of Talpidae—the mole family—that may add their own variety of spadework to your soil. All of them have the same basic pattern: stocky body, practically no eyes or ears, short legs and forefeet built like shovels. They also have fur that rubs either way, without any "grain."

The star-nosed mole (*Condylura cristata*) has twenty-two

fleshy-pink "fingers" that surround its nostrils and feel the way as it moves forward. Its relative the common mole (*Scalopus aquaticus*) has a long slender proboscis that can probe around like a stubby elephant trunk. Brewer's mole (*Parascalops breweri*) has a more conventional snout, but sports a hairy tail instead of the scaly or naked tails of its cousins.

It is no accident that the two ends of a mole bear such unusual adornments. The sensitive nose probes for worms and crickets and beetle grubs. So does its tail, when the animal is in reverse. And a mole can travel backward as well as forward, since its fur will lie flat in any direction. Otherwise all its tunnels would have to have a little turntable so it could switch ends to get back where it came from.

One further word about those tunnels. They are scarcely beautiful, but that's from *our* standpoint. To the mole they are, of course, life itself. Surprisingly, they are almost that to the lawn as well. A mole tunnel with its loose, porous roof gives perfect entrance to rain from the slightest shower. Not only that, but the tunnels serve as little dams, holding surface water and greatly slowing down runoff. On sloping soil they act as tiny terraces, sometimes preventing disastrous erosion.

Still, there comes a time when you wish the moles would carry on their wonderful deeds elsewhere. It does little to recall that the moles helped make our rich topsoil what it is today. Our feeling is that now that they have come this far, we'll be glad to take over. And so we toss poisoned peanuts in their runways, blow cyanide in their burrows, jab electric probes into the ground. Since the sense of vibration is second only to that of smell for a mole, we also put children's pinwheels on the lawn in hopes the flying vanes will jar them right off the premises.

Then, if these fail, we may employ that barbarous device known as the harpoon trap. Poised over a runway, it drives lethal spikes downward when it is tripped. Sometimes it gives a quick kill, but it may catch only a nose or a foot. Then the mole must wait hours, sometimes days, until the sprung trap is noticed.

One way of catching a mole alive and unhurt consists merely of taking advantage of its weakness. As it is practically part of the soil itself, this little plug-along has little sense of gravity. Coming to a cliff, it might well burrow right over the edge and fall. So, just create your own "cliff." Provide something to catch the animal, and there's your mole.

Start by stomping down all the runways you can find. The ones that are soon pushed back up are the active ones. Dig a hole in such a runway large enough to take a three-pound coffee can or similar container. Bury the container deep enough so its rim is flush with the floor of the tunnel. Cover it with a board or loose vegetation.

The mole comes snuffling along, intent on repairing its runway. It falls into the can, has no means to climb out, and waits to be rescued. Unearth the can and take its occupant off where it can dig undisturbed.

Quite different from the stodgy mole, but placed close to it in the biological scheme of things, is that accomplished aerialist, the bat. There are several kinds of bats that may visit anything from a suburban tool shed to the dim galleries of a city museum. None of them poses a threat to your well-being, but few people are able to keep their equanimity when one is around. A bat that blunders into a room—or even swoops low over a park bench—may trigger an elaborately offhanded shrug, a hasty exodus, or a frantic chase with a broom.

Such antics on our part are understandable. After all, we are products of our upbringing, just as is the bat. To daytime beings like ourselves, creatures of the night are mysterious and somehow evil. Nor does the erratic, doubling-back flight of the bat make you feel any easier; the critter looks as if it is bereft of its senses. Then, too, if you ever get a close look at its features you lose the last of your confidence. The best of our local bats looks like a tiny bulldog. The rest of them look like something left over from a grade B horror film.

Of course the bat was scarcely built for our edification. The big ears and pug nose allow it to hear echoes of its supersonic squeaks and snap up the insect that produced the echo. The fluttery flight is explained by the fact that at the end of each flutter there's an insect. The presence of a bat around your head at an evening barbeque is likely due to the same cause. After all, we attract mosquitoes and gnats; they just naturally come to many of our outings. So, in reality, the bat that attends your picnic in the park may well be doing you a favor as it snaps your small attendants out of the air.

It's this fondness for insect life that sometimes brings these misunderstood mammals into a building at night. Insects attracted by the light may be followed by bats attracted by the insects. If a door or window is left open the bat may willingly enter it. After all, bats *do* live in caves and hollow trees.

The best procedure in such a fix is to allow the little creature to make its way out again. Its superb echolocation sense will quickly reject foreign objects such as walls, lampshades and people until it finds the door. Wild flurries with a broom or folded newspaper only confuse and excite the bat. They don't do much for the people, either.

Bats, of course, will not get in your hair. Nor, except in rare cases, have they been known to carry disease. About the worst of their effects is simply that they are *there*. And "there" can mean some surprising places, if you only knew about them. For instance, an unused chimney is a fine place for a bat to hang itself up in after a night on—or above—the town. If a fireplace or stovepipe hole is open, the creature might end up in the room. Attics are favorite haunts, too. So are the dim recesses in the roofs of outbuildings.

Bats really *do* inhabit belfries, by the way. The quiet and lofty recesses of a church steeple make fine dormitories. One time my friends Everett and Nell Skinner invited me to visit the bell tower of Riverside Church in New York City. We went up during a morning concert. We watched in fascination as the great carillon pealed out a stirring hymn. Then I noticed that the bells had another audience—hanging within inches of all that clamor were three little brown bats, peacefully sound asleep.

Bats have been found as extra globs of "paint" clinging to the works of old masters in dim museum archives. They sneak into the ends of piles of lumber and fly out when the boards are taken off. Their massed flights, emerging from the ground like smoke, led to the discovery of Carlsbad Cavern. Once a bat added a touch of realism to one of my slide presentations. I had given a wildlife program, shown the last slide, turned up the auditorium lights, and there was the bat, swinging back and forth over the heads of the audience in a ghostly encore.

With such an active life, the bat has certain domestic problems. Although it is largely crepuscular—flying at dusk and dawn—a bat may be away from home all night. Those Carlsbad bats travel twenty miles or more to their feeding grounds each evening. A city bat may find its livelihood in the suburbs, or vice versa. However, instead of foisting the young off on others—as the cowbird does—or bringing back enough extra food to last a day or two—as the wolf does—the bat takes its youngsters along.

Baby bats cling to their mother's fur for a couple of weeks, or until they're weaned. Sometimes the female has only one young; other times she may have four. For obvious reasons, such a quartet of burgeoning batlets may gain its wings in a hurry.

While many languages refer to the bat as a flying mouse, the true mice are quite different creatures. The bat has greatly elongated fingers that serve as a framework for its wings—hence, *Chiroptera* ("hand winged")—while the mouse and its rodent relatives have more conventional paws. Sometimes the four digits function remarkably like our own, as when a mouse or squirrel sits up and holds a seed while it nibbles. It usually lacks a thumb, however. That handy addition to our hands is often merely a nubbin on the side of a mouse's foot.

The term *rodent*, by the way, comes from a Latin word that means "to gnaw." And gnawing is what these animals do best. They *have* to be good at it; their teeth are growing constantly, every day of their lives.

Those familiar rodents, the mice, come in a number of sizes, temperaments, and effects on their human neighbors. The little deer mouse (*Peromyscus*), with its warm brown upper fur, snowy-white underside, liquid-dark eyes and large ears, is one of the most appealing of the clan. As you survey the effect of those sharp incisors on the jacket you hung in the garage, you can almost forgive the little critter for making a nest of clothing scraps down behind the paint buckets. And, when you go to clean out the nest box in the spring for this year's birds, you're liable to close it up hastily if you find it filled with a deer mouse's fluffy nest. "After all," you tell yourself, "the mice have to live, too."

One of the many virtues of the deer mouse is its thrift. Virtue, that is, if you look at it from the standpoint of the mouse. Seeds, cherry stones, peach pits, nuts and raisins may be spirited away to a hidden storehouse. Sometimes an entire bird feeder is cleaned out overnight. The industrious rodent may filch every sunflower seed and spirit its treasure away where you'll never see it again.

Well, almost never. But in my case it was different. And all on account of my writing habits.

The machine on which I'm typing these words is an ancient Underwood No. 5. Born in 1923, it's an old upright

Deer mouse

desk model—cantakerous now, and noisy enough to sound as if I were typing on sheet metal. But I bought it secondhand for five dollars, and in spite of Peg's complaints I refuse to part with it until I've gotten my money's worth.

We had been away for a week and had put the fabric cover on the typewriter to keep out the dust. When I returned, rarin' to write a best seller, I whipped off the cover, sat down to type—and there was not a sound.

Nothing would work. The typewriter was incommunicado. One glance told me the story: finding the machine to be dark and silent, a deer mouse had filled the type-basket with birdseed. So full, in fact, that at my first effort at typing several dozen seeds rattled down through the mechanism and on to the desk.

Further search uncovered more seeds: behind the books, in the drawers, in the file cabinet. Even an old pair of slippers held its share. The only place without seeds was the windowsill feeder. We had filled it before we left, and apparently the mice got there before the birds.

We cleaned the typewriter, dumped out the slippers, and returned the seeds to the feeder. Soon I was back at my best seller. But, score one for *Peromyscus,* who had shown an abundance of that priceless quality an animal must have if it's to live with people: the ability to make a change.

While deer mice usually inhabit brushland and fence rows and little wooded plots, their relatives the field mice live in grassier areas. "Danny Meadow Mouse," as Thornton Burgess called him, is a chunky creature with uniformly gray-brown fur, short tail and ears, and beady eyes. Strictly speaking, Danny is a vole, a distinction that need not bother us here except that it means the 4½-inch rodent is related to the famous migratory lemmings of the North.

Meadow mice often do the damage for which the moles get blamed. Gifted with an appetite for nearly anything in the vegetable line, they'll follow a mole runway and shear off nearly every root they find. If no moles are handy, the mice make their own tunnels. Burrowing through matted grass, leaf litter, or even through the snow, they make a maze of pathways. Often you'll see a round hole in the snow where *Microtus* has tunneled up for a look around. Later, as the snow melts, the paths form a lacework there on the golf course, the garden plot or the grassy strip of the boulevard.

Less rustic surroundings are preferred by the house mouse (*Mus musculus*). Gray-brown above, with a lighter underside, this mouse has tossed its lot squarely in with people. Occasionally it takes up residence in an abandoned quarry or trashy area, but it is soon back in civilization. From its nest of soft material in a wall or under a trunk it forages for our scraps.

One time a friend of mine was standing at a subway platform. "There was a commotion down on the tracks," said Carol Krieg, "so I walked in that direction to see what was causing it. And there were two mice in the middle of a squabble. They'd stop and fight, and then run, and stop and fight again."

She watched the running battle until her train rumbled in. "And when last I saw them they were still at it."

That train, doubtless, shook their battlefield. The mice, however, didn't seem to mind. Indeed, so well have subway mice adjusted to their noisy, shadowy surroundings that they have been there, generation after generation, since the first subway was built.

Why isn't the subway overrun with mice, since so many mice are down there without any enemies? Simple: they *do* have enemies.

In the first place, there's hunger. While apple cores and hot dog rolls make good eating, there's a limit to litter. Even the offerings dropped through the street grating above cannot sustain the mice forever. At some point there's not enough to eat, and new families of mouselets will starve.

Secondly, there are the cats. Sometime after the subways were started, a wandering domestic tabby discovered that the tunnels made perfect places to prowl. Others of its kind came to the same conclusion. Soon the catacomb cats settled in on a permanent basis. They've been there ever since, never seeing the glimmer of daylight from birth until death. They make a living on *their* available food—the mice and rats around them.

You can occasionally see one of these creatures from the door at the end of a subway train. A furtive figure crosses the tracks, perhaps, or a shadow detaches itself from the gloom beyond a dim bulb. And there's your glimpse of an underground microcosm—a macabre machine run by the motive power of forsaken popcorn, abandoned sandwiches, and the other ejecta of subwayites.

The rats of the underground have their counterparts in the buildings above, of course. If the starling and house sparrow are paragons of success in the bird world, the mammalian honors would have to go to the Norway rat. Estimates indicate that there is a rat for every person in America.

Such a figure, of course, is but a guess. *Rattus norvegicus* seldom stands around to be counted. However, U.S. Department of Agriculture figures point out that, no matter how many there really are, our rats cost each man, woman and child a dollar a year. And that's a dollar you've *got* to spend, whether you want to or not—in packaging, food losses and disease.

The reasons for such accomplishment are several. In the first place rats share the general rodent flair for begetting more rodents. I recall well a male white rat I had in seventh grade, for instance. White rats are merely an albino variety of the common household type. Thinking my pet might be lonely, I got him a mate.

Things went wonderfully. Alfred and Alfreda hit it off from the first. In a little more than three weeks we had half a dozen pink, blind youngsters the size of bumblebees. My school classmates were delighted. Although two of the litter died, the survivors were eventually taken off to four homes.

In honor of the two parents, these youngsters were all given names beginning with A.

Just about the time we disposed of the last of the litter, Alfreda presented us with seven more. Every one of these lived. Their names, we decided, should begin with *B*. Feeling that I had some kind of gold mine at hand, I sold the seven for a dime each. So, in just two months I had parlayed two rats into thirteen—plus seventy cents.

Just as I was congratulating myself that the money would almost pay for the food, litter C arrived. There were only three in this group—which was lucky, because there were no more takers. In fact, I had to take back three of my earlier rats because the parents of Earl Roy and Lonny Thompson didn't understand rats very well. Or maybe they did. At any rate, I realized I had better call a halt to the enterprise until I had disposed of my present stock of six young and two adults. So I separated Alfred and Alfreda.

That, however, was not enough. Within a few weeks the returnees from the Roy and Thompson homes were old enough, too. I realized this when I found four babies in their box.

Twelve rats, now—and the local market glutted. Alarmed, I hastily divided my broods before they ran right down the alphabet. Then I called a local high school. Could the biology teacher use a dozen rats representing three generations? Luckily, he could. So I managed to peddle my pets all in one afternoon. But I had had enough of population explosions before I had ever heard of the term.

Beside such prowess as being able to reproduce when only three months old, the common rat possesses other abilities. It can make its home almost anywhere—cargo ships, cargo planes, old buildings, new buildings. It inhabits forgotten cars, packing boxes, dumps, sewers—even the "thatch" of old vegetation high on the trunk of a stately palm tree.

I remember watching a rat crawl along a hawser linking a freighter with a dock in Baltimore. The hawser had a conical metal rat-guard to prevent such a transfer, but this did not hinder the adventuresome rodent. Perhaps by accident, perhaps by design, it slipped off the thick rope and fell into the water. Then it swam ashore.

Add to such an adventuresome nature an almost uncanny ability to avoid getting caught. Set your most clever trap right in a rat's favorite haunts, and the chances are that it will scorn your best efforts and make a detour. Or else it will steal the bait without springing the trap.

It seems to thrive on most poisons, too. Even the chemical warfarin, which acts on the blood, has its limits. Wise old female rats will sometimes pass it by. And even if it's working fine, when the numbers of rats have diminished enough, you forget to put out more. This, of course, allows the whole affair to build up again.

But not even Brother Rat, there in the cellar or down along the waterfront, is a villain all the time. Laboratory rats have served us well in the study of nutrition and genetics. Many of our diseases have yielded to research with their aid. Fledgling scientists solemnly probe into the internal workings of preserved rats in countless classrooms. Then, too, you can get wonderful affection and entertainment from one of these creatures as a pet. But recalling my grammar school experience, I'd warn you to get just one.

The Norway rat, by the way, probably did not originate in Norway at all. Actually, *Rattus norvegicus* has been with us so long that nobody is sure exactly where it started. But, no matter who sent it to us, this redoubtable rodent brings with it in a one-pound package all the gifts and talents that city animals need so much these days. And all those gifts can be summed up in that single word you've heard before: adaptability.

Take another rodent, for instance: the squirrel in the park. Whether it's the frisky gray squirrel (*Sciurus carolinensis*) or the larger and more sedate fox squirrel (*Sciurus niger*), there's that flexible streak that helps them *stay* in the park. Acorns and nuts were their original food; now many a squirrel survives on popcorn, peanuts and other provisions doled out by friends on a park bench.

Squirrels can also make at least part of a living on animal food: insects, snails, and the eggs of unfortunate birds. One squirrel in Providence, Rhode Island, has worked this variation in the menu for all it's worth. The squirrel lives in trees at the edge of a shopping center. The cars that park near its home are met by this one-rodent welcoming committee. Leaping from the weeds at the edge of the macadam, the squirrel bounds up to each new car as it arrives.

It's not a peanut or cracker that the squirrel is anticipating, however. Carefully inspecting the headlights, radiator grille and bumper, it finds what it is seeking—insects crushed against the front of the car.

Its nesting habits allow for change, too. The young are ordinarily born in spring in a leaf-lined den in a hollow tree. However, if no suitable site is found, nests of leaves are made in the tops of other trees. You've probably seen these shaggy nests high in a fork over your head.

Then, following an impulse with which we are all familiar, the mother squirrel apparently changes her mind. Perhaps the neighborhood has deteriorated, or perhaps she just finds another spot that suits her better. At any rate, she may move her family two or three times before the babies are grown.

Sometimes fleas and mites get to be too much of a challenge. She hauls her three or four youngsters off to another location, leaving the pests in full control of an empty nest.

Tree squirrels are also good at escaping other enemies. Frighten a squirrel, and it circles around to the back of the tree trunk where it cannot be seen. Get a friend to go around to that side so you've caught it in a cross fire, so to speak, and it takes refuge in a crotch, or even flattens out on a horizontal limb while you're still looking for it up in the branches.

Peg and I have played host to several gray squirrels. Some have been fully wild ones that have learned to rob the bird feeders; others have been brought to us because they were orphaned or wounded. One in particular was a male squirrel whose mother was caught by a cat as he was being carried to a new nest. Although free to come and go as he pleased, Sparky stayed with us for more than a year.

Sparky went with me on my lectures and accompanied us on woodland hikes. He would ride on a shoulder for a while; then he'd jump up into the branches, keeping pace with us from tree to tree. Sometimes he would pause to investigate a nut or a pine cone, but soon he'd catch up, taking incredible leaps from limb to limb or even across the open space over a driveway if we were walking in town.

Sparky had little use for cats or dogs. He would scold and spit and chatter at even the most docile pup. If we were on a stroll and he discovered a dog or cat he'd go as close as he dared and hurl insults from a handy tree or bush.

One day his stream of invective went too far. A little terrier objected to Sparky's language and jumped right up into the bush from which the squirrel had been launching his verbal attack. Sparky panicked and raced across the lawn, followed by the irate terrier. With a frantic leap he hit me in the chest and scrambled to the top of my head.

The terrier, now fully aroused, did the same. Or he tried to. And from the sound of *his* language, if I wouldn't give up the offending squirrel, he was going to come up and get him. So I did the only brave and sensible thing—I panicked, too.

There was a car parked at the curb. Luckily it was fairly

old and battered. However, its condition didn't really matter. It was obviously my turn, so I leaped.

And there we were: me on the hood of the car, Sparky on my head—both of us treed by a twenty-pound terrier.

I don't know how it would have turned out had not the dog's owner come to the rescue. However, she saw the scene, and whistled off her wolf pack. Then, graciously forgetting to laugh, she admired the little rodent that had caused it all. As I said before, squirrels can be resourceful critters. And on occasion their owners don't do so badly, either.

Resourcefulness has allowed that perky little ground squirrel, the chipmunk, to keep right on doing business at the same old stand, so to speak. Chipmunks are normally woodland animals, and have seen their backwoods turn into back yards. They normally live in underground burrows, with emergency shelters in the form of decayed stumps or hollow fallen logs. They seem to know to the nearest inch just how many leaps they are from safety at any moment.

Now the 'munks still dig the burrows, but their modern escape plans include such refinements as storm sewers, culverts and old barrels. Once I saw a chipmunk completely outwit a cat in a pile of six-inch drain pipes. The pipes had apparently been dumped there in preparation for some project that had never been completed.

The chipmunk seemed to know every pipe end perfectly, even if the pipes were in a jumbled heap. It would pop into a pipe just ahead of the cat and run to the other end. Then it would sit there and chatter until the cat was almost upon it. Sometimes for variety, it would quietly duck right back into another pipe and reappear within a few inches of its pursuer.

The unsuccessful feline endured this new version of cat and mouse as long as it could. Then, in that snooty way that cats have, it turned its back on the whole affair and regally stalked away. "If you won't abide by the rules," it obviously said with a disdainful flip of its tail, "we're not going to play at all."

If a chipmunk can keep free of entanglements with cats, dogs, snakes and predatory birds, it may spend much of its time in that typically squirrelish activity, gathering nuts and seeds. Whereas the tree squirrels are apt to poke a nut into any convenient spot in a lawn, the 'munk fills one or more hideouts with several gallons of seeds. Cheek pouches allow it to carry half a handful at a time. With the onset of winter, it retreats to a deeply buried cache, curls up with its beloved seeds, and drops into the semideath of hibernation.

Every few weeks the little rodent stirs itself. Awakening, it yawns, perhaps scratches a somnolent flea, and turns its attention to the food supply. Then, having raided its wintry icebox, it drops off to sleep again.

The chipmunk's portly cousin, the woodchuck, stores its food in a different fashion. The groundhog, as it is also called, puts away its provisions in the form of fat. A friend of ours, Dr. Ruth Young, whose trim proportions belie her interest in such things, has discovered that *Marmota monax* can put on weight just about as fast as any living mammal. It can go from a svelte six or eight pounds to a pudgy ten or twelve in just a few weeks.

This may not sound like much, until you realize that it is just about doubling its weight. And even that may seem to be a ho-hum fact until you realize something else: only a small amount of that weight is for the groundhog's winter sleep.

Most of that fat, it seems, is necessary because these creatures are early risers. Early in the year, that is—any time from January to the end of March. But no matter when they arise, there will scarcely be any new greenery to eat. You and I will not have planted our tasty vegetables yet. Airports, country clubs and cemeteries still wear the brown of winter. Even the grass on the median strips, road banks and cloverleaf intersections—favorite haunts of today's superhighway woodchucks—will supply little that's fresh and new.

And so that busily chomping creature has to lay in a store of food more than half a year ahead of time. Thus, as it's grazing in your summer garden, it's really having the meal that will be denied to it next spring. Which, as you survey your ravaged crops, is a comforting thought indeed.

Actually there *is* a bright side to the antics of old whistle-pig. (That name, by the way, comes from its habit of uttering a shrill whistle when alarmed.) Most of us seem to enjoy the groundhog legend. And, apparently, so does the groundhog. It wakens from hibernation several times during the winter. Occasionally such a fit of insomnia may bring it briefly to the surface of its burrow on February 2. We eagerly scan the roadsides, the "rough" along the golf course—or the TV screen, with its report about the national groundhog in Punxsutawney, Pennsylvania—to see how long this cursed winter has to go.

The national groundhog, at least, usually sees its shadow—if only from all the flash cameras recording the event. This frightens it back into its burrow. The nation relaxes, with its weather well in the care of the slumbering rodent.

There's another undeniable "plus" to woodchucks. They are active during the day. You have a good chance of seeing at least one woodchuck for every five miles along many of our interstate highways. There will often be one or two in the no-man's-land of the cloverleaf, too. And such a large creature along the roadside could well provide that touch of wilderness that we all need to keep our computerized lives in balance. Besides, even if that scurrying form that crossed the highway *wasn't* a bear, it's nice to speculate that it *could* have been.

Groundhogs, being rodents of generous proportions, make burrows of commensurate size. Such burrows are often appropriated by other animals for homes when the original owner moves out. More than fifteen mammals have been known to use groundhog dens as nest sites. Foxes and coyotes enlarge them to suit. Rabbits, raccoons and porcupines may find them just right. Chipmunks, ground squirrels, other rodents, weasels, skunks, shrews and opossums help round out the list. In the days of the timber wolf, even *Canis lupus* might refurbish an old groundhog home at the edge of a woodland or on a favorable hillside.

A frantic animal, fleeing a grass fire, may find its life saved by a convenient woodchuck burrow. A rabbit, dodging a hawk or a dog, may pop down into its welcome depths just in time. So, not only is the "wejack," as the Indians knew it, an adaptable creature by itself, but its home allows all kinds of animals to occupy it in a sort of continuous game of Outdoor Musical Chairs.

Other rodents may occasionally make their homes in town —or, at least, in the suburbs. Muskrats may harvest the cattails and rushes in some swamp that has not yet fallen victim to the drain-and-fill syndrome. Their houses, made of reeds and mud, look like low mounds in the water or along the shore. Now and again you may find a muskrat feeding platform of mud strewn with bits of uneaten reed, plus a mussel shell or two. As an added fillip, *Ondatra zibethica* may deposit a few musky-smelling pads of fecal material, just to establish ownership.

Also aquatic, but unable to stay long when people move in, is the beaver (*Castor canadensis*). The dam-building activity of this twenty-pound rodent usually gets it in trouble. Its ponds are necessary to help it float tree branches to a point where they can be stored in the mud for the winter. They also supply protection for the web-footed rodent. However, they flood farms and roads and valleys. So, although the fortunes of America were built on beaver pelts, the big, peaceful creature seldom gets to share long in its heritage.

Rabbits, to most people, are just another form of rodent.

Scientists say that they are not, however; their teeth are different. Bona fide rodents have four incisors, two up and two down. Rabbits have an extra pair of uppers. This little difference, plus other peculiarities, places the rabbit and its cousins the hares in a separate group of mammals—the order Lagomorpha.

The cottontail rabbit, scooting along the edge of a field or dodging among the bushes of an abandoned lot, may seem a fragile creature at best. However, it too has learned to survive almost everything we toss at it, short of a slab of concrete. Any respectable-sized city park can probably boast at least a few cottontails. So can many other little bits of wilderness that occur in most cities. *Sylvilagus floridanus* and family can get along on less than an acre of ground—in other words, on an area smaller than a football field.

On an evening stroll you may see that white powder-puff tail bounding away though the dusk. If you noted the spot where it originated you may find one of the reasons for the rabbit's ability to cope: its vaunted ability to provide more rabbits. In a shallow nest, lined with the mother's fur, may be half a dozen little cottontails.

Although born naked and blind, the babies grow at an astonishing rate. Their eyes are open at a week; they're running around at two. In three weeks they have left the nest and are on their own.

Meantime, the mother is well on the way toward producing another brood. Given the chance, she probably mated the same day her first litter was born. About a week after they leave the nest she brings four to six more youngsters into the world.

Fortunately, this pace does not keep up forever. Her last brood may have been born in early autumn. Then there seems to be a halt to reproduction. But with the coming of spring, she's back in motherhood again.

The cottontail can accept almost anything green to help

charge its perpetual-motion battery. Clover, dandelions, plantain, alfalfa, garden vegetables, your best flower border—the list is endless. And, as with Peter Rabbit and his briar patch, prickly shrubs seem to be no problem. Indeed, a rabbit may nip off the top two feet of every raspberry and blackberry you have.

Occasionally a fox moves in to help keep the rabbit population in limits. Foxes are more common than you may think. When we lived on Long Island we used to watch a vixen and her pups at the edge of the Bethpage golf course. The three pups were as playful as their domestic cousins, and would romp all over their mother until she had to get up and move. Sometimes they would creep up on her like a cat stalking a bird. If she wasn't around they'd stalk a beetle, or even an ant. They'd toss a bone in the air and run to catch it.

It was hard to realize that we weren't watching a litter of everyday puppies. However, just the slightest warning from their mother would stop them in their tracks. We assumed she made some special sound, although at our binocular distance we could hear nothing. Then, at another signal, they would scoot for the den and tumble out of sight.

With her keen eyes, nose and ears, she doubtless knew that we were watching her. Apparently we became too familiar; one day the den was empty. There was no sign of a struggle. Inspecting the spot, we found just a mound of earth surrounding a hole in the sandy soil. We had once seen the father bring a squirrel for his family; only a single well-chewed bit of gray fur was left. But we hoped that, wherever the little family had moved to, there would be plenty more squirrels, with perhaps fewer binoculars, and fewer golfers beating the bushes after a lost ball.

Foxes have been known to live near playgrounds and public picnic areas. The town dump used to be a favorite hangout too, before the day of the sanitary landfill. And the ten-pound little trotting dog with the luxuriantly bushy tail usually knows the location of every Lover's Lane. Such a spot is a gold mine of half-eaten hamburgers, french fries, and maybe a partly occupied milk-shake cup after a good Saturday night.

A regular visitor to such areas, too, is that ring-tailed little gleaner, the raccoon. Possessing not only an anything-goes appetite for everything from a steak bone to a soggy ice-cream cone, the raccoon is also gifted with the ability to find such delights no matter where you toss them. Put the garbage in the can where it belongs, and put the cover on tight; chances are that you will hear the cover go clattering before you're out of earshot.

Two raccoons began to visit the back yard of some friends of ours. "We were delighted at first," Bill Potter told me, "and we put out scraps for them. However, one night we went away without putting out any food. When we got back, the garbage pail had been upset and there was rubbish all over the yard." Obviously the garbage pail hadn't been securely covered. Cleaning up the mess, they put the cover on tightly. Then they put out some more food and went to bed.

"But now that they had found the can," Bill said, "they wouldn't leave it alone. In the morning things were right back in the same mess. So my son and I put a big stone on the lid of the can. 'There,' we told ourselves, 'let's see them figure *that* one out!' "

They figured it out, all right. The can was open, the garbage strewn, just like the night before. So Bill and his son waited up with a flashlight to see how they did it.

"And, by gosh, it was simple," Bill reported. "Those raccoons merely pushed on the can until they got it rocking. The stone rolled off, and they were into the can in ten seconds."

Not that the little bandits had figured things out, of course. Quite likely they had pushed petulantly on the forbidden container the first time. The slightly domed contours of the cover and the uneven shape of the stone had done the rest. Being raccoons, they took advantage of a good thing. Then they merely repeated the process the next night. And, sure enough, it worked.

Raccoons are like that. Abundantly and continually. They have been known to untie a bag of suet hung out for the birds —not break the rope or chew it in half; untie it. They have figured out the turnbuckle on many a chicken-house door. And, denied entrance to an abandoned building by regular means, they have pulled off a screen and opened a window. Or else they've gone up to the roof and come down through the chimney.

Anyone who has had much experience with raccoons can tell you more stories. Those black little handlike paws, the sharp teeth, are forever probing, testing, trying. Sooner or later the string comes untied and the suet falls to earth. The latch opens—and there are all those delicious chickens. The intriguing smells of an unoccupied building just naturally invite exploration.

Since a raccoon can climb, run, jump and swim, it can usually figure out *some* way to solve its problem. Small matter that in so doing it creates half a dozen new ones. Raccoons like a challenge, anyway.

Loosely translated, the raccoon's scientific name, *Procyon lotor,* means "the pre-dog that washes." It often washes its food before eating, but such a performance is not at all necessary. We have been foster parents to eight raccoons, but none of them washed its food all the time. Nor, on the other hand, did they merely wash things that were dry or dirty. Two of the foods that get the most frequent sudsing by raccoons are fish and frogs.

Why does a raccoon wash its food, then? We'll probably never know. After all, we cannot explain our own actions

Raccoon

much of the time. But, I figure, it's sort of like a baby playing with its oatmeal—it just feels good.

The fifteen-pound "aroughcun," as Captain John Smith translated the Indian word for it, is gifted with an outsized curiosity. Watch a raccoon at a streamside or in a bevy of old cans and bottles; it pokes its hands into every hole, turns over every stone. Such curiosity will turn up many food morsels that more lethargic creatures would miss. Even as we held any of our own animals in our arms, their little fingers would be investigating a ring, a wrist watch, the button on a sleeve. And all the time that little black-masked face would be peering about, apparently considering what mischief to get into next.

Raccoons can nest almost anywhere. All that is needed is a quiet sanctuary. The hollow of a tree is ideal for the birth of up to half a dozen babies in the spring. However, an overgrown culvert will do almost as well or—as happened in the dump at Chincoteague, Virginia—an abandoned piano.

A midnight telephone call from a lady in Burlington told me of a raccoon on the second floor of her apartment building. When I went there the next day I found that mama raccoon had been climbing up the ivy on the chimney outside the building, entering through a loose clapboard, and raising a family under an old-fashioned bathtub in an empty apartment.

Such persistence and ability to "make do" are good Vermont traits, of course, so the raccoon was right in line with the best tradition. The lady sealed off the room so there would be no more apparitions in the hallway. And so, chalk one more up for durable, pliable, mischievous Ringtail.

Less of a scamp than the raccoon is that plodding, good-natured little wood kitty, the skunk. Related to such opposites as the playful otter and the formidable wolverine, the skunk yet has a personality all its own. Poking along over your lawn in its ceaseless search for grubs and mice, it is at peace with the entire world.

Unlike many peacemakers, however, *Mephitis mephitis* (which, naturally, means "poison gas poison gas") backs up its demands with a terrible weapon. It never uses the weapon except in self-defense, for the skunk doesn't like the smell, either. But so intent on its errand in life is the nearsighted little eight-pounder that it may blunder into trouble at any moment.

Puttering along in pursuit of a meal, a skunk may find a tasty tin can by the side of the road. Poking its head into the tin, it licks the contents clean. Then, trying to back out, it makes an unnerving discovery: the jagged edge of the tin refuses to allow its head to come free. In plain language, it is stuck.

I received an emergency call on just such a skunk early one Sunday morning. Changing to my oldest clothes, I drove to a nearby town to see what help I could give. Nor did I have to inquire where the skunk was; it clattered right up the middle of the town's main street, backing into parked cars, the curb, utility poles.

Luckily, there were few cars yet on the street, so the skunk had not created a traffic problem. Walking up to the little creature, I began to speak in what I hoped was a soothing voice. The skunk stopped, turned, and raised its head—can and all—in my direction. Still speaking, I reached down and scratched the pavement a few feet away from the skunk. Then, continuing to scratch so it could hear the noise approaching, I placed my hand on the tin can. The little captive shivered, but held its ground.

As far as I could see, the can had no ragged splinters that might cut the skunk. Apparently the only thing really sticking was its fur. I eased my hand off the tin onto that rich, glossy fur. More shivers, but I still spoke words of great balm and comfort. Then, taking hold of the can with my other hand, I yanked. Off went the can. Away went the skunk, head over heels. It looked at me a few moments; then turned and trotted off beneath a hedge and out of sight.

I was relieved, but not surprised. Skunks would rather have things nice and easy, all around. I have had my hands on three other wild skunks, with squirt guns all intact, and have yet to be sprayed.

Incidentally, a skunk can spray from almost any position,

and with anything from a fine mist to a jet that may reach ten feet. And, in case you find one in your garage, don't believe the old story that it cannot harm you if you pick it up by the tail. Sometimes those anal scent glands are closed by the act of lifting, true. But sometimes they aren't. And, besides, how are you going to let it go again?

The best course of action, as with nearly every creature that visits, is just to let it find its way out again.

Incidentally, if you, your cat or your dog *are* sprayed, tomato juice makes a good neutralizer. Clothing hung in the air soon loses its aroma, too. The oil is highly volatile, and fades away in the hot sun. Burying the clothes accomplishes nothing. Except getting rid of them, of course.

Skunks themselves hardly smell skunky at all. They are neat and clean in their personal habits. Unless they're in dire straits, they do not spray if there's a chance the spray will blow back onto themselves. So a mother skunk, puttering along through your back yard with four or five babies in single file behind her, is scarcely cause for worry. Unless you're a grub or beetle, that is. If you leave them alone, all you'll see in the morning is a few little holes in the lawn, each marking where some insect met with its destiny.

And there they are—'possums in the parking lot, bats in the belfry, skunks out by the swing. Not an impressive army, I suppose, compared to wolves and mountain lions and moose. But they are a source of interest—and all the more exciting when you find them because, in our nine-to-five lives, such creatures seem to have no place.

Yet they *do* have a place, of course: in their world and in ours. For perhaps half the population of our continent today, the sight of a 'possum, blinking in the lights of a parking lot, can be a wonderful bit of therapy. Such an adventure may be almost as much thrill for us there, deep in civilization, as meeting up with a bear in a bunkhouse off in the backwoods.

9 · *Welcome Mat*

ALL RIGHT, THEN. You spot a wisp of green poking up through the sidewalk. A solitary sparrow lands for a moment on your window box. A skunk seems to be thinking of taking up residence beneath the front stoop of that old house where it won't bother anybody. How do you encourage them? How do you spread out the welcome mat—and keep peace with your neighbors at the same time?

That last question is perhaps the most important. Neighborhood zoning ordinances—or just common sense—may advise you to go slow. That gentleman next door who works the night shift may not appreciate a bunch of birds yammering for their food at daybreak. The lady with an herb garden probably has a few ideas about skunks that dig little holes in the soil. And if the old sidewalk is due to give way to a new shopping center, you might as well save your time and effort.

Suppose, however, that it is all right to encourage that little bit of greenery or bird or animal life. Realizing that every case is different, what suggestions can be made that will work anywhere, anytime?

Actually, the suggestions are only two. And they can be wrapped up in a single sentence. Every living thing, whether it wears fur or feathers or foliage, must be supplied with two basic needs: food and shelter.

For our purposes, let's assume that the term "food" includes water. In plants, it also includes the soil that nourishes the roots, plus the airborne gases that feed its leaves. Shelter is of several types, too: the right balance of sun and shade to a plant; protection from the winds; protection from pollution; a place where its seeds may sprout and grow.

Shelter for animals may encompass a place to eat, to sleep, to mate and have young, to escape from enemies. It also takes in what might be termed "territory"—or, as we would call it, elbow room. Given these essentials in the right amount, there's a good chance for almost any plant or animal.

Consider the little seedling in the crack in the sidewalk, for instance. You probably cannot help it much until it's moved to more advantageous surroundings. This involves elbow room and the proper balance of growing conditions.

Without knowing what kind of plant you have, of course, you can't very well guess what it will need. But there are a few suggestions that will at least tip the scales in its favor. Some of these have already been mentioned—getting as much soil as possible with the roots; having the plant face in the same direction with regard to the sun as it was when you dug it up; using plenty of water with transplanting; and putting it in the same relative amounts of sun or shade.

Stake the little plant up if necessary: this will keep it from being whipped by the wind. The stake will help you find it later when the weeds are tall—unless, of course, you want it to remain hidden. Use a strip of cloth to tie the plant to the stake so as to allow room for growth. The cloth will rot in a few weeks, letting the plant stand on its own. You can make a waterproof identification marker by writing on an ordinary tag and covering it with cellophane tape.

Pull the weeds nearby to lessen competition. Strew them around the base of the new arrival. They will help conserve moisture, inhibit the growth of further weeds, and supply organic material as they rot into the soil. Kitchen vegetable scraps will help, too: carrot tops, potato peelings, onion skins. They will slowly decay in a little on-the-spot compost pile.

As long as you're transplanting, you may wish to know whether your plant will be attractive to the birds. Most evergreens provide fine shelter, but produce little nourishment until they're old enough to bear cones. Deciduous trees and shrubs may afford little shelter in winter, but their fruit and berries are useful as food. Red berries are especially attractive —both to you and to the birds. Modest amounts of fruit that remain on the twig through the winter are better than an abundance that falls with the first freeze.

If your enthusiasm takes hold and you decide to try your luck at converting an abandoned lot into a minipark, a few more suggestions might come in handy. Use native plants where available. Perhaps some are growing there already, and merely need to be given a chance. Be slow about removing them until you're sure what they are.

Other plants may be found nearby, all adjusted to the climate and soil and the peculiarities of your city air. They have another advantage, too: they're free.

Often a wide mixture of plants will have more success than just a few types. This makes for visual interest while it lessens the pitfalls where there is little variety. Consider what would happen to your carefully nourished elm grove, for instance, if Dutch elm disease got started.

There's another drawback to having just a single species or two. Take the hardy ginkgo tree (*Ginkgo biloba*) as an example. It's an Oriental import of venerable ancestry. Through the ages it has developed an immunity to practically every hazard of life, including the smoke and grime of cities. You'll see its peculiar fan-shaped leaves borne along some of our busiest streets—New York's Riverside Drive, for instance.

However, it's hardly the species for your neighborhood park. Not if one of those you plant is a female tree, at least; the plumlike fruit smells terrible. Get it on your clothes or shoes and you'll be asked to leave the house. And until your trees get large enough to blossom you'll not be sure of which sex they are.

The variety in your vest-pocket park can include a dead tree or two. Such old-timers, often hollow, are an invitation to nesting birds and small mammals. They'll attract insects, as well, plus the creatures that feed on them. Almost every bird that visits the park will land on the dead tree sooner or later, right where you can see it. Besides, a gnarled old stub adds interest to the scene.

Overgrown fence rows and roadside strips form good avenues for both food and shelter. Old stone walls and overgrown banks allow creatures to move from place to place without exposure. Such places naturally have a wealth of many kinds of greenery. Cemeteries are good places of refuge, fenced in and quiet. Old foundations can often harbor a number of animals.

If the land has any slope at all, or if one side is more sheltered than the other, you can try the old gardener's trick of improving on the weather. Plants that are less hardy or are from Southern regions should be put on the sheltered portion, or on a slope that faces south or west. Tougher types can get along on north-sloping, shadier, more exposed areas. Sometimes you can persuade a plant that normally exists as many as three hundred miles further south or north to grow right where you want, merely by choosing the right spot.

As you prune and clear brush, save what you have gathered. Brush piles make fine shelter for rabbits, birds, and—if you can take them—snakes. Leaf mulch is good for snakes too, or bad for you, depending on your viewpoint.

There's another reason for saving brush and twigs. The tastiest buds and foliage can often be found at their ends, out of reach of ground-dwelling creatures. In the woods around my Vermont home, the deer have learned to come to the noise of a chain saw. Usually the sound means that a tree is being felled. Soon there will be delicious treetops to eat. In fact, one common wildlife-management stunt is to cut trees and let them lie where the animals can work at them.

Another practice is that of providing extra homes for wildlife. Not just bird boxes—which we'll consider shortly—but caves and dens and hiding places. A fallen hollow log makes a good cave. So does the space under the roots of an upturned tree. Neither of these may exist, however, on that little plot of ground. So, add a few of your own.

One rock propped up on another makes an acceptable shelter. So does a carefully placed clod of earth, a board, even a slab of bark—anything under which a small creature can hide. Unused culverts or soil pipes make good caves, especially if one end is partially blocked. In fact, in your initial cleanup of the place, go slow in removing the debris that's already there. Some of it may harbor the very creatures you're trying to attract. Remember my snake in the beverage can.

If birds are your interest, don't scorn the common sparrow or a few starlings. They may well serve as decoys. Birds feeding will attract other birds. We have often noted that a flock of starlings will contain a red-winged blackbird or two in winter. A single goldfinch may consort with half a dozen sparrows. Apparently the occasional stray seems to share the feeling we all have on occasion: there's safety in numbers.

Not only the shrubs and trees that bear fruit, but the weeds that hang on to their seeds during the winter will serve as food Buds and even the tips of twigs may be snapped off by birds with husky beaks—the finches and grosbeaks. Tight clusters of pine needles may house slumbering insects, and loose bark on trees may be a winter dormitory for many kinds of creatures. Keep an eye on such places; they may serve as natural bird feeders.

A friend of mine goes out every day and spreads a mixture of peanut butter and cornmeal on the trunks of several trees around her house. Thus, when a bird comes along one day on its routine inspection of the bark, it finds the bonanza. Soon it is coming regularly, and her wildlife boarding house has acquired a new customer.

Other creatures will also respond to such an invitation. The aroma of peanut butter attracts animals just as it does people. Tree squirrels may visit the sylvan smorgasbord. Mice, opossums and raccoons will help themselves.

Since you're dealing with a few strands in the living web of the outdoors, other "strands" may become evident, as well. When the birds get especially numerous around our feeders, a hawk or shrike may move in for a few days. It enjoys easy pickings until the birds become wary. Then, usually, it moves on. Other predators—snakes, shrews, possibly even a weasel—may come to the feast as well. So may the neighbor's dog and nobody's cat.

This brings up a point that's often misunderstood. When you feed the birds or animals, the inclination is to put the food where the creatures will be sheltered from the weather as they eat. Thus, many a feeder is carefully located near a protective evergreen. The bread crusts are tossed out by the base of the tree so as to temper the force of the wind. Such situations, however, should be avoided if there are potential enemies about. Otherwise you may be leading your small visitors right into a trap.

Better to put the food out where there's good visibility in all directions. Then nothing can sneak up undetected. Winter winds and snow and rain are normal to the lives of wild things, anyway. In fact, except for times when there's a howling storm, the gray and drizzly days are often the ones with the most going on at the feeder.

Our feelings about the weather, it seems, are not necessarily *their* feelings about the weather. It's like that definition of a sweater, I guess: something a small boy wears when his mother feels cold.

Care and feeding of wildlife is as much a matter of "when" as it is of "what" and "where." Peg and I maintain our feeders around the year. However, many people feel that summer-fed birds are probably shirking their job of looking for insects. Our thought, in putting out food on a sunny afternoon in June, is really twofold: perhaps the parents will bring their offspring to the feeder where we can watch them; and we hope they'll stay in the habit until next winter.

Sometimes a squirrel teaches her young to climb by introducing them to one of our feeders. Juvenile squirrels, it seems, are as shaky as a movie comic on a fire escape when they first leave the nest. But, coaxed by their mother, they soon learn to perform the simple deed of climbing the pole of the feeder for the delights of the waiting sunflower seeds. From there they graduate to tree trunks, then to limbs, and finally to full-scale acrobatics.

Once you start putting out food for wildlife, you should not stop. Not abruptly, at least—especially during the winter. Of course, if your "feeder" is a natural little area where you have encouraged trees and shrubs and seed-bearing weeds, the food will normally taper off until there is scarcely any left. But it is a disservice to a creature to cut off its daily handouts because you're going away for a week, say, during the holidays. After it has become dependent on you it may find it impossible to forage for itself.

The critical period in the lives of many birds and animals is the end of winter, when most natural food is gone and new supplies have not yet begun to grow. In those dreary weeks you may decide to chuck it all and head for Florida. Turning your back on your wildlife at that time is scarcely better than kicking your dog out in the street. Better not to start a feeder at all than to close up shop and head south just when the creatures need you most.

The kind of feeder you use is limited only by your imagination. One of my most memorable was merely a square of plywood with little slats of wood around the edges to keep the seed from spilling off. No roof, no sides, no rudder to swivel it into the wind.

My feeder was tacked onto the outside windowsill of our house. There was no natural shelter in any direction for forty feet. Thus its visitors could feed at their ease without the hazard of unpleasant surprises. Provisions were easily added, too; I merely opened the window and put out the day's rations.

The birds and animals didn't care how fancy the feeder was, of course. All they cared about was the food. Over a period of nearly four years I loaded several hundred pounds of seeds onto that flimsy square of plywood, one handful at a time, summer and winter.

My roster of guests included forty-seven species of birds, nine mammals, a snake and a frog. Not all exactly at the feeder, I admit, because it was about six feet off the ground. But several creatures poked around beneath it for scraps.

The birds were some of those that are so blithely shown on the bags of birdseed as if they were everyday visitors. Among these were a scarlet tanager, several catbirds, a pair of orioles and a rose-breasted grosbeak. Warblers paused in their migrations. One summer a hummingbird came daily to the feeder's single embellishment: a pill bottle filled with red-colored sugar water.

The mammals included a family of gray squirrels plus a flying squirrel that glided to a soft landing from a distant tree while we watched enthralled at dusk. There were also two kinds of mice, several opossums and a pair of raccoons.

One day a chipmunk was peacefully gleaning scraps from the ground beneath the feeder when a shrew pitched into it. The shrew might have won, too, if it hadn't missed its first jump by a hair. By several hairs, actually; it launched its attack on the chipmunk's tail. That appendage broke off under the nip of those sharp teeth. The curtailed chipmunk fled, leaving the shrew in possession of four inches of furry brush.

Where did that busy piece of plywood receive all those visitors? In my present adopted town in rural Vermont, perhaps, or on my boyhood farm in western Connecticut? Hardly. My no-cost-it's-the-upkeep feeder was nailed on the outside of our home in Massapequa, New York. The Long Island Rail Road shook the place several times a day. Cars roared and screeched past almost around the clock. The reason for the feeder's success was an overgrown, swampy area behind the house. The swamp meant mosquitoes; but these meant birds and other animals. Mosquitoes are to a swamp what grass is to a meadow: they are the base for a whole pyramid of life.

In contrast to that feeder is one in the yard of some friends of mine. Made of redwood and selling for about twenty dollars, it's built like a little house. The seeds come out the bottom onto a platform as the birds use them up. Two walls of the house are of glass to show how many seeds are left. When the supply gets low you fill it through the chimney.

What makes this feeder unique is a balanced perch on which the birds must land to feed. A small bird can easily reach the seeds, but the weight of a larger bird causes the perch to swing down like a seesaw. This drops the bird out of reach.

Sparrows, finches, redpolls and chickadees have no trouble with the feeder at all. Jays, grackles, starlings and similar large birds, however, find themselves frustrated. One jay, nevertheless, has solved the problem: it hovers in front of the feeder on flapping wings like a big, clumsy hummingbird. It gobbles as many seeds as it can, right in midair, until its wings give out.

"I'm just waiting for that jay to teach the same trick to the others," Travis Harris told me, "and there goes twenty bucks."

There are dozens of devices and gadgets to foil the big birds while the smaller birds eat free. You can get satellite feeders that tilt and ferris wheel feeders that whirl. Feeders with entrance holes too small to admit anything larger than a sparrow. Feeders that dole out their rations from the bottom just for the benefit of small clinging birds. One feeder a friend saw has a big, fake owl that springs out at the psychological moment. It's triggered by a switch and run by a battery.

The main idea, of course, is to separate the large birds from the small. Thus they all get to eat. The simplest way I've found to sort them out is to use the principle you may remember from your sandbox days: sift them through a strainer.

The sieve you'll use is a coarse mesh fencing known in some hardware stores as turkey wire. Its strands are laid at right angles and welded together to give a one-by-two-inch mesh. Raised a few inches over a platform or above the food on the ground, it allows the small birds to drop down through, while larger birds can be fed elsewhere. Pinch adjacent strands together to enlarge the rectangular openings a bit if necessary. And there, for a dollar or so, you can accomplish as much as somebody else's high-priced feeder. Then you'll have all that extra money for bird food.

You can take a plastic bottle or a milk carton, cut a couple of 1½-inch holes in its side, and you've just made a feeder. You've recycled a bit of waste, too. Scalp the top off a coconut, hollow out the meat, and you've got a rustic container for seeds. More recycling.

A friend of mine with a couple of spare automobile hubcaps decided to recycle *them* too. He tacked them to a block of wood in such a way that, when hung up, one would be the roof and the other the platform of a feeder. Thus he has a gleaming counterpart of the popular gadget made of two wooden bowls separated by a dowel. "Dinner by Detroit," he calls it.

A coffee can with a plastic lid makes a good feeder, too. Cut half-inch notches in the rim with heavy shears. Place the can on one of those throwaway pie tins. Fill the can with seeds, snap on the plastic top, and you've got a recycled self-feeder. The seeds come out as needed through the notches. If you don't care for the advertising on the can, give it a coat of paint.

The point is to save a container that will hold enough food so that you're not running back and forth all the time. Paper cups hung by a string; glass jars inverted over a plate so you can see how much food is left; even pine cones daubed with peanut butter make acceptable feeders. (That peanut butter, by the way, should be mixed with cornmeal, birdseed or raw oatmeal; otherwise it may become impacted in a bird's tiny innards, or at least cling to the roof of its mouth just the way it does to yours.)

Drill a few one-inch holes in a chunk of wood and fill the holes with the peanut-butter mixture. Or merely find an old stick with a knothole, dab the mix in the hole, and hang it up for the birds. As for birdseed itself, there are many mixtures. Experiment until you find a combination that seems to fit the tastes of your own birds. After several days of feeding, note the seeds that are left. Then try to get a mix that has few of that kind of seed next time.

Sunflower seeds are universal favorites. They're expensive, however, so buy them in quantity with several friends, if possible. Get the smallest ones you can: there are more of them to the pound, and they last longer.

A chickadee or a titmouse will take a sunflower seed to a branch, hold it between its feet and whack away until it has picked out every morsel. Finches, cardinals, grosbeaks and sparrows will sit right on the feeder and shell the seeds out on the spot. Jays may either open the seeds to get the meats or may just gobble them up, one after the other. That's when you appreciate that turkey-wire screening.

Put out orange halves for summer birds such as tanagers, cedar waxwings, thrushes and orioles. Raisins are good, too. Don Lattrell, at the local supermarket, saves ancient fruit for me in a box labeled "O.K. for Ron Rood." Birds eat the flesh of melons and pears, while squirrels, mice and chipmunks relish the seeds. The outer leaves of lettuce make a welcome bit of greenery in winter.

One of the best and cheapest foods is beef fat, or suet. It is especially relished by insect-eating birds. The more firm and chunky this suet is, the better. The best suet is that flaky fat found around the kidneys. It holds together well and is slow to melt on a warm day. Ordinary cuts of fat disintegrate under the influence of the sun until you have your own little oil slick, there on the back porch.

Hang a chunk of suet in one of those mesh bags used for packaging lemons or onions. Or make a container out of that coarse screening known as hardware cloth. Tack the container to a solid support if you want to feed all comers, from jays to chickadees. Hang it from a string if you'd rather just have the small clinging birds and woodpeckers. Jays, grackles and starlings will still pick at it, but they are rather clumsy at such acrobatics and may become discouraged.

Sometimes we "try out" or melt down a batch of suet until it's liquid. Then we stir birdseed and raisins into it until the whole affair is like a grainy soup. Pouring it into an empty milk carton, we let it solidify. Around Christmas time we top it with a maraschino cherry as an added personal gesture.

When the suet-seed-raisin mixture has hardened, we peel

away the milk carton. There stands a big, cubic "candle" with a red-cherry "flame" that will attract several species of birds at once. Depending on the weather and the bird and animal traffic through our yard, each one-pint chunk should last at least a couple of weeks.

Gravel is appreciated by birds, especially if there is snow on the ground. The hard particles are used as grindstones under the muscular action of their innards. Birdbaths are more useful in summer than in winter and should be placed where the birds can watch for enemies as they bathe.

In locating your feeder, take a note of the weather. Figure out the direction that brings the worst winds and locate your feeder in the lee of a somewhat distant tree or building, if possible. Note the shape and location of snowdrifts. Watch the places where the rain drives hardest. Usually next to such areas there is a zone of relative calm. By feeding birds in such a zone you can take advantage of a natural, but invisible, shelter.

More substantial shelter must be afforded if you hope to persuade your visitors to remain and raise their young. Besides those caves and culverts and thickly foliaged plants mentioned earlier, some special nesting structure may be needed. Robins, phoebes and barn swallows usually build on a shelf or horizontal limb. Merely make them a platform in a sheltered location. We have several such ledges of plywood about eight inches square up under the eaves of our buildings. Some are used one year, some another.

Most nest boxes are made, obviously, for hole-nesting species. But that is no sign that they'll use them. A house wren I knew raised a brood of young in the crown of a hat in a tool shed. I once took photos of the occupant of a wood-duck nest box with its four-inch hole. The box was a home for a tree swallow that could almost fit through the hole sideways. And a structure I put up for bluebirds was

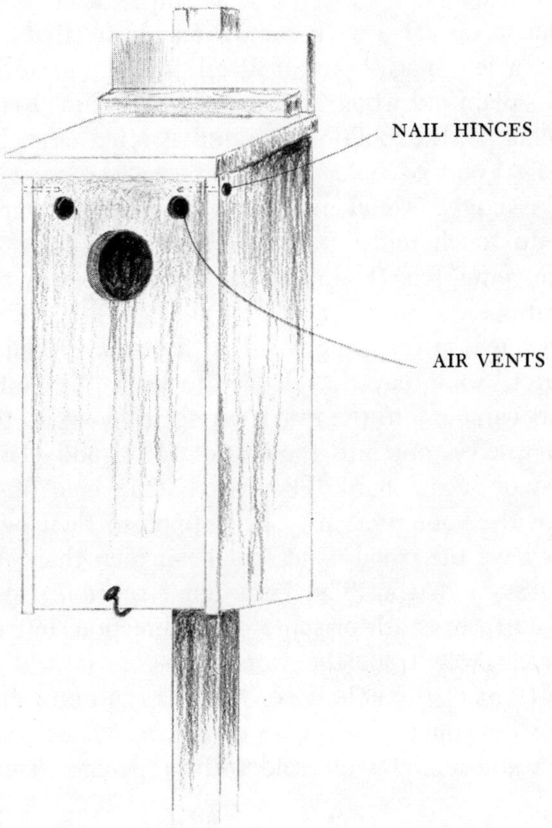

Bluebird house

see text for other details

preempted by a white-footed mouse—who was evicted by a chipmunk.

The point, as I said earlier in this book, is that birds and animals do not read the rules. But, still, a wren house is a better bet to attract a wren than is an old felt hat.

Hence, a few suggestions. If at all possible, make the box of wood—plain old wood, with or without paint. Keep away from metal, plastic, roofing paper and assorted other building materials. Wood is cooler on a hot day; warmer when the weather is chilly. Metal and many artificial substances get too hot to touch under a blazing sun. They'll fry the unfortunate youngsters. They also get clammy-cold as the temperature drops.

Another reason for using wood is that you're dealing with living birds. Some day they'll have to leave the nest. Their tiny claws can cling to the rough surface of wood so they can boost themselves out into the world. Metal and plastics are usually smooth and hard. They need some kind of interior ladder, or the youngsters may be trapped in their own nest.

Better have the wood at least half an inch thick. Paint it or not; it's up to you. The birds don't seem to care. Face the box north or south or some other direction, but it's best to point it away from the worst rainstorms. Add a little perch in front of the hole if you wish; it's more to make the bird pose for you than because of any real need. After all, knotholes and hollow stubs seldom have perches right below the hole.

Scores of books give dimensions for bird boxes. But remember: the box is an imitation of nature. No two tree holes will be alike. As a general rule, however, the box should be deeper than it is wide. The entrance hole should be far enough below the roof so the fledglings can get out without banging their heads. Yet it should be high enough to allow for a good, well-built nest.

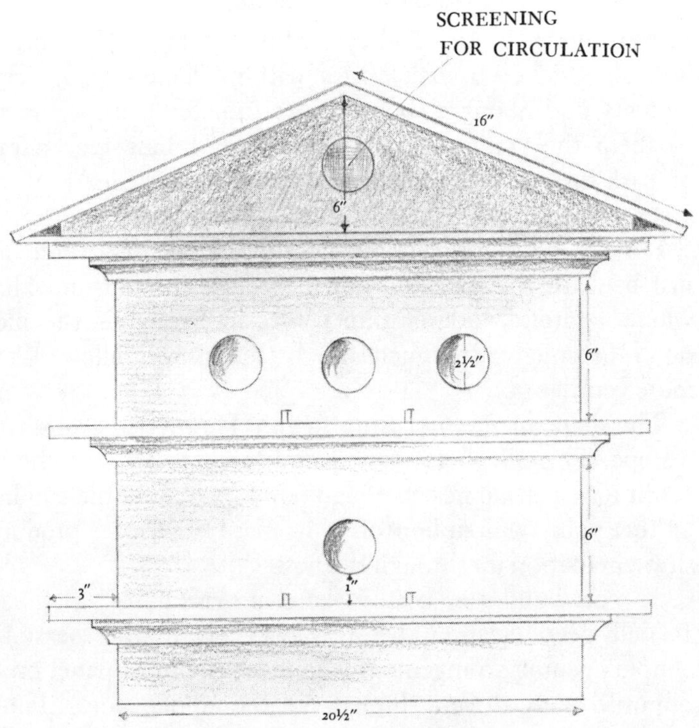

Purple Martin House

One leaflet on my shelves gives instructions for more than fifty boxes and platforms for nesting birds. Yet, remembering the ridiculous little tree swallow in the huge wood-duck box, I believe that one or two sizes will actually be used by any bird that needs them. Provided, of course, they're not already occupied.

Bluebirds, chickadees, tree swallows, wrens, titmice, nuthatches, house sparrows and house finches will all use a house with inside dimensions of 5 by 5 inches in area and 8 inches high. The approximate metric equivalents are 12 by

12 centimeters in area and 20 centimeters high. The entrance hole should be an inch and a half in diameter (3.7 centimeters) and about 2 inches (5 centimeters) from the top. To help the youngsters leave the nest, I may tack a piece of bark or a square of screening to the inside for that vital first step.

Provide ventilation or drainage by means of several holes just beneath the roof and down through the bottom. Here's where amateur workmanship comes in handy: if the pieces don't fit snugly, so much the better; they'll allow all the more ventilation.

The shape of the roof is up to you. However, be sure it has a slope. This allows for runoff and tends to localize the hottest internal air up near the high point. A few ventilation holes at this point will siphon off this air. They'll also produce a slow circulation up through the nest.

As you build the box, make a provision for opening it. It will need cleaning before each new nesting season. A simple opening arrangement is to pivot the front panel on two opposite nails driven through at the upper sides. Thus it may be swung up and out for cleaning. Lock it at the bottom, either with an *L* screw, a cuphook bent to shape, or a couple of nails driven in and clinched over to hold the panel shut.

The entrance hole itself, if exactly an inch and a half in diameter, will accommodate the small birds but will not admit the starling. Just an eighth of an inch larger, however, may allow a starling to enter, while a two-inch hole is ideal for this larger bird.

Put out any number of bird boxes. Don't expect them all to be used, however, even if there are plenty of birds about. That "elbow room" for house sparrows, say, may be only a ten-foot circle. Bluebirds, however, may need a five-hundred-foot radius. Other birds may be allowed to nest nearby, yes—but no more bluebirds for five hundred feet.

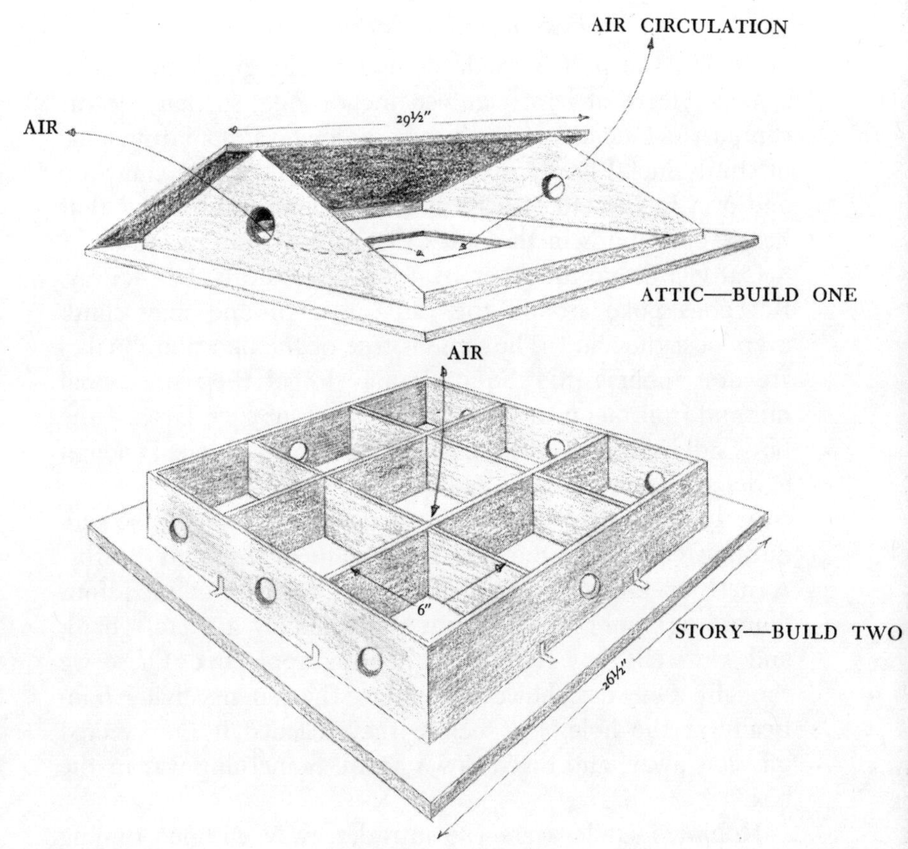

Purple Martin House

Nest boxes can be placed anywhere. The birds may use them more readily, however, if they have good visibility. Thus a box on a post may be used, while the same box, half hidden in shrubbery, might remain empty. Birds appreciate a view, I guess, just as we do. Besides, it helps them note the approach of enemies.

Speaking of enemies, it should be a law that no bird box may be put up without a cat guard on the post. Unless, of course, the post is made of metal. The guard should be a metal sleeve at least eighteen inches long, so that the cat cannot reach across. It can also be a downward-pointing cone of sturdy metal firmly fixed, so that the cat cannot climb up and over it. Place it at least as high as your head. A cat that hears young birds in the nest can set new jump records.

Cat guards are for other creatures besides cats, by the way. Raccoons poke around the yard at night and may climb every post they find. The same is true of the opossum. Snakes are nest robbers, too. Squirrels may forget their traditional nut and fruit menu to muddle up a batch of eggs. Even if the birds survive such a visit the parents may be frightened enough to desert the nest.

As long as you're putting a cat guard on the pole be sure nothing can reach the box from some high point nearby. A nest of bluebirds we had on our lawn contained four flourishing young ones. It was protected by a metal guard, and was well away from a neighboring apple tree. Or so we thought. One day, however, we saw the parents flying frantically at the hole. Just before they reached it they veered off, flew away, and dived down again. Something was in the box.

Hoping I could scare the intruder away without ruining the babies that might still be unhurt, I tapped gently at the post. Instantly a little face looked out at me. Two rounded ears twitched in my direction. A pair of saucy eyes surveyed me a moment. Then, with an explosive chatter, a red squirrel shot out of the box in a leap that carried it halfway across the lawn.

How had it managed to get into that box? Simple—the nearby apple tree had grown since the last time I had thought about it. One limb stretched out toward the box, tempting the squirrel to try a leap. Obviously it had made it, too. All four babies were dead in the nest.

Another hazard of nesting is brought about by our efforts to be helpful. Birds appreciate nesting materials such as string, feathers and strips of cloth. However, be sure you cut the string in pieces about six inches long. As it picks at longer pieces, the bird may get caught by a wing or a leg.

One of the perils facing birds near fishing areas is the fishline stripped off the reel and thrown away because it's tangled. The bird gets caught in a loop as it walks along the shore or attempts to pick up the line for its nest. Eventually it strangles, or gets snagged in a bush, or is impaled on the fishhook.

Assuming, however, that such tragedies do not happen and you've managed to attract a few birds, how can you get to know them better? That sparrow was the first one to pay a visit; how can you persuade it to come again? Or, if it has been there several days, how can you help it get used to you? Suppose you're trying to befriend a chipmunk; how do you go about it?

The main thing is your attitude about it all—your attitude, that is, from the point of view of the bird or animal. Consider that angle, and there are several things that you may do a little differently. In the first place, wild creatures are immediately suspicious if you pay them too much attention. A steady, direct stare—that's the way a hawk behaves just before it strikes. Better look away frequently, or even watch your visitor out of the corner of your eye. If you move about, make your motions slow and deliberate. Try not to go in the creature's direction. Or, if you do wish to get closer, travel sideways while busily watching something else.

And don't swallow. Swallowing, after all, is the last act the bird or animal wants you to perform. More than once I've carefully zeroed in with my camera on a nervous bird. Getting close on tiptoe, as it were, I have accidentally swallowed—and got a beautiful surrealistic picture entitled "Flight."

To take a wildlife picture (and these suggestions also apply to other wild animals beside birds, by the way), have everything ready. Everything: camera shutter cocked, proper exposure and shutter setting figured; potential distance set on the lens; camera up by your face ready to glance into the finder. Now, sneak up in your indirect act. Look out toward Hawkins's house while you gradually sidle toward your subject. Then, when you're near enough, just turn your body in one smooth motion and shoot.

In talking with another person in the presence of a bird, just use a low tone of voice. The ears of birds are tuned to high-pitched noises, such as the sibilant sounds of whispering. Many birds may not be able to hear your normal voice at all.

In watching mammals, you probably will need to go on the graveyard shift. Most of them are much more active at night. Canned dog food makes a good meal. So does bacon and peanut butter on whole-wheat bread. Put the food in several pans to eliminate squabbles. This may be important in case you have a skunk or two in the crowd.

In watching the animals, use a light with a red bulb. They do not seem to notice it at all. Flash pictures, surprisingly, hardly bother them. Neither does the low, soft-speaking human voice.

In another book I have made suggestions as to the care of orphaned or wounded creatures. Generally, however, you will get along with them better if you adopt that calm, casual attitude. They're apprehensive enough already. Remember, as far as the little what's-it is concerned, you're a predator. So it's up to you to show that you're not.

Creature comforts first: warmth, dryness, perhaps a little nourishment if it can eat without being forced. In other words, give it food and shelter. Let it see that you obviously have had plenty of chances to do it in, but haven't harmed it. Then, after its mental attitude has changed and it has become used to you, work on that fishhook or that torn ear.

Any bird or animal will repay efforts made in its behalf—especially as the city gets bigger and the countryside gets smaller. Even a tiny pond can be made a better, more interesting place. Those two needs for food and shelter are important to fish and frogs too.

Bushes allowed to grow along the edge of a stream or pond will shade and cool the water. Insects from their leaves will fall in as food. Birds will land in their branches and void their droppings in the water. Thus they'll help make it more productive. A pond gets its nourishment from the soil, just as a pasture does. Indeed a proven method of raising fish production in a pond is to dump fertilizer into it.

Overhanging banks help to shelter many water creatures. So do submerged logs, hidden stumps, jutting rocks. Turtles can use a log to bask on and an open sandy spot in which to lay their eggs. A clear, clean pond may be nice for wading, swimming or canoeing, but it is limited in aquatic life. There are more fish and pollywogs around that old tire, likely, than out by the sandy beach. Indeed, one way to dispose of old tires nowadays is to hitch them together and drop them offshore. They form an underwater "reef" that soon becomes rich in marine life.

Not that we should joyfully roll all the abandoned tires into the nearest pond, of course. But an inert tire, lying there on the bottom, *does* contain a nice, circular "cave" about six feet long. It's a fine spot for little fish to hide in and for larger fish to snap them up. Dinner by Detroit, again.

You can help the inhabitants of a little brook by encouraging those streamside bushes for shade. A log dropped across the brook will create a little pond, complete with waterfall. Bubbles in the tiny cataract aerate the water. Where the current scoops out the soil and gravel below the log it stirs up aquatic organisms. Thus it helps the food chain. Not only that, but the waterfall looks and sounds pretty, too.

Drop in a stone here, a log there. They'll create swirls and eddies. You can use them to guide the force of water away from an eroding bank or toward the inside of a curve. Again, they add food and aerate the water. They also create interest, and they look good.

A part of such a stream is owned by a friend of mine. The total length of his portion of the stream is less than a hundred yards. When he bought it, the stream was just a long, uninteresting series of shallows. By dropping six logs across at selected intervals, he created six little pools. He allowed the vegetation to grow along the banks of these pools, shading the water.

Now, although he hasn't ever stocked the waters, there are dace and minnows and even an occasional trout in that brook, where not a fish existed before.

Yes, many of them are doing well, these plants and animals. Some of them get along because of us; others in spite of us. But if you look around, and listen, and regard that crummy old vacant field as something besides a crummy old vacant field, you'll find that it's teeming with life. Or it could be, with a little encouragement.

And—who knows?—maybe there's a possum in *your* parking lot, too.

Index

Italic page numbers indicate illustrations.

Index

Index

F

G

H

I

J

K

L

Index

Y

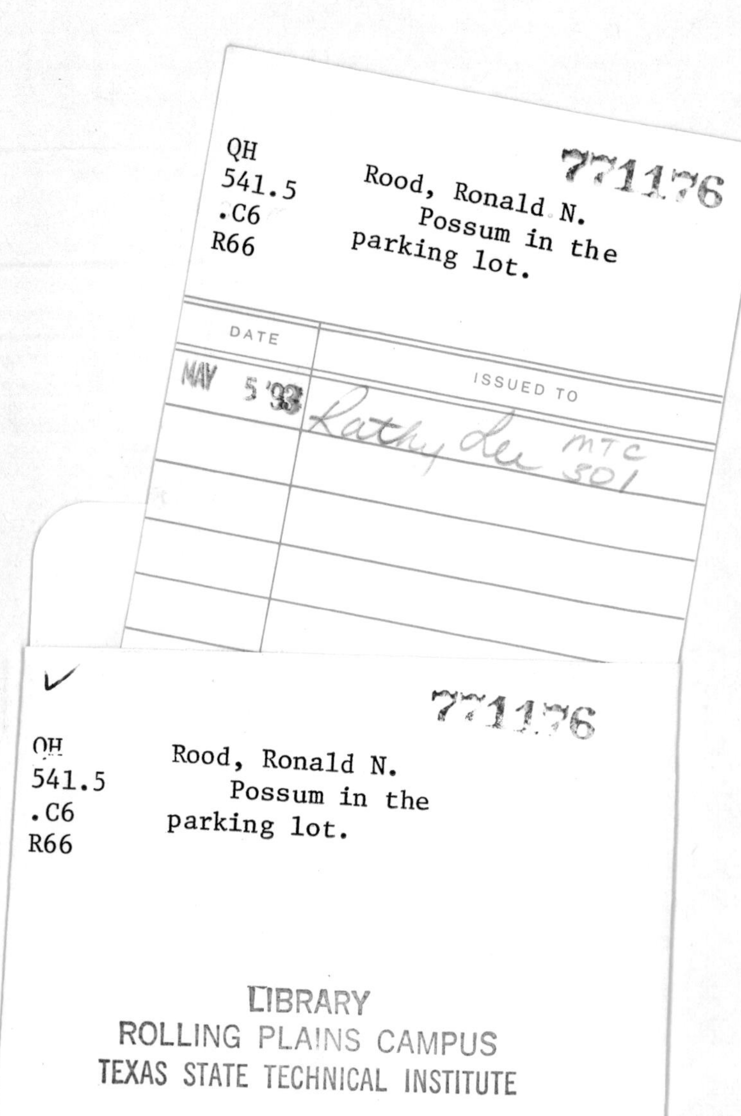
QH
541.5
.C6
R66
771176
Rood, Ronald N.
Possum in the
parking lot.
DATE
ISSUED TO
MAY 5 '93
Kathy Lee MTC 301
771176
QH
541.5
.C6
R66
Rood, Ronald N.
Possum in the
parking lot.
LIBRARY
ROLLING PLAINS CAMPUS
TEXAS STATE TECHNICAL INSTITUTE